BEDTIME MEDITATIONS FOR KIDS

A COLLECTION OF MEDICATION TALES TO HELP KIDS BEING AWARE OF THEIR BREATH, GO TO SLEEP CALM AND BEING GRATEFUL.

Table of contents

BEDTIME MEDITATION FOR KIDS

Bedtime gives a mysterious fateful opening to meditate with children. This progress in the calendar is now set up as a time when we quit playing, drop the hecticness of the day, and set up our brains and bodies for unwinding, resting, and in the end, for rest. Meditation, in like manner, is predicated on relinquishing entrusting and settling over into calm reflection. A large number of us with small kids additionally have entrenched, pre-bedtime schedules, so slipping a three to brief meditation into this example is moderately clear.

Of the huge number of meditations, children will, in general, take to Metta, or lovingkindness, on the grounds that it is visual, coordinated, and conjures warm fuzzies. Practising loving kindness with my two children when they were preschoolers and dozed in a similar bedroom. I didn't anticipate quite a bit of a reaction. However, they cherished it and inevitably didn't feel their bedtime routine was finished without rehearsing metta daily. Indeed, even in later years, in the event that we wound up dozing in a similar space, for example, in a tent or lodging, our kids requested that I lead a Metta meditation before resting.

With small kids, keep Metta meditation short and basic. In its most essential structure, Metta can utilize three expressions:

- May __ be sound

- May __ be sheltered and ensured.

- May __ be upbeat and tranquil.

The three expressions are applied to classes of individuals:

- Oneself

- Someone with whom the kid has a cozy relationship, for example, a relative, instructor, parental figure, or companion

- A creature or part of the common world, for example, felines, pandas, streams, or mountains.

- All creatures, all over the place

Don't hesitate to adjust this any number of ways. You can alter the expressions and increment the classes depending on your kid's formative limits. For instance, you can include Metta for individuals we don't have a clue, for troublesome individuals, or for networks experiencing a cataclysmic event. (Understanding meditation educator Gregory Kramer's booklet Seeding the Heart is an extraordinary asset for working with various age gatherings.)

In spite of the fact that in my family, we rehearsed Metta while cuddled into our beds, my companion Nilakshi and her four-year-old child sit together at their family special stepped area.

He lights incense and rings the ringer himself. Their picked classifications are themselves, one individual in the family, somebody from the more distant family, one companion in school, and one sort of creature. She imparted to me that she cherishes, seeing him grin when he picks the individuals to offer Metta to and that he is typically quiet when he heads to bed directly after.

For your initial barely any nights, you can utilize a content (like the one beneath) until you get its hang. At that point, make the structure that works best for you. Before you start, have your kid pick which relative or companion the person in question might want to send lovingkindness to, just as one component or creature from nature.

In the wake of rehearsing this for half a month, your kids should lead the meditation themselves. Awesome—put it all on the line.

METTA MEDITATION FOR BEDTIME SCRIPT

- (Speak the accompanying for all to hear.)

- Take a long, full breath in, beginning route down in the midsection. Topping off, up, up! What's more, enormous breath out—"AAAH!" (Make a noisy murmur with the breath out.) And once more, long breath in, topping off, up, up! Also, once more, our moan of alleviation—aaaah!

- Now, loosening up our bodies, letting them become delicate and substantial, simply softening into the bed, feeling warm and comfortable. Everything totally loose. In the event that you need, you can put a hand or two hands on your heart. We should feel our hearts and picture a warm, shining light, similar to daylight, that is transmitting from our heart community outward. This heart daylight gleams with affection and benevolence.

- Let's start with generosity for ourselves, recalling our own essential goodness and graciousness. (You can make reference to something from the day, as well, for example, "Emma shared her Legos and Connor cleaned up the feline barf, despite the fact that it was overly gross.")

- Think of these expressions in your brain: May I be sound. May I be sheltered and secured. May I be upbeat and quiet. (Portray each line gradually. Respite for at any rate 5 seconds between expressions to permit time for the youngster to envision or feel the association and expectation.)

- Now we share our lovingkindness with grandmother. We should picture grandmother in her preferred seat in the daylight by the window. May grandmother be sound. May grandmother be sheltered and secured. May grandmother be upbeat and quiet.

- And they are letting our Metta emanate outward to the rainforests of the world, with monster trees giving natural air to us to breathe and obscure overhangs and homes for a huge number of types of creepy crawlies, creatures, and clans. May all rainforests be sound. May all rainforests be sheltered and ensured. May all rainforests be glad and tranquil.

- And then emanating consideration, over the whole world, spreading upward to the skies, and downwards to the profundities, outward and unbounded.

- May all creatures be solid. May all creatures be sheltered and secured. May all creatures be cheerful and serene. (Whenever wanted, include, "May all creatures be stirred.")

GUIDED MEDITATION FOR KIDS

Fun Ways To Teach Your Kids Mindfulness

1. The Bell Listening Exercise

Ring a bell and request that the kids listen near the vibration of the ringing sound. Instruct them to stay quiet and lift their hands when they never again hear the sound of the chime. At that point, instruct them to stay quiet for one moment and give close consideration to different sounds they hear once the ringing has halted. After, go around and request that the kids disclose to you each stable they saw during that minute. This exercise isn't just enjoyment and gets the kids amped up for offering their encounters to other people; however, it encourages them to interface with the present minute and the affectability of their recognitions.

2. Breathing Buddies

Hand out a toy to every youngster (or another little item). On the off chance that room permits have the children rest on the floor and spot the soft toys on their guts. Guide them to take peacefully for one moment and notice how their Breathing Buddy goes here and there, and whatever other impressions that they notice. Instruct them to envision that the musings that come into their psyches transform into air pockets and buoy away. The nearness of the Breathing Buddy makes the meditation somewhat more amicable and permits the kids to perceive how a lively movement doesn't really need to be boisterous.

3. The Squish and Relax Meditation

While the kids are resting with their eyes shut, have them squish, and crush each muscle in their bodies as firmly as possible. Instruct them to squish their toes and feet, fix the muscles in their legs as far as possible up to their hips, suck in their stomachs, press their hands into clench hands, and raise their shoulders to their heads. This is an extraordinary, fun movement for "releasing up" the body and mind, and is an absolutely available approach to get the kids to comprehend the craft of "being available."

4. Smell and Tell

Pass something fragrant out to every youngster, for example, a bit of crisp orange strip, a sprig of lavender or a jasmine bloom. Request that they close their eyes and take in the fragrance, centering the entirety of their consideration just on the smell of that object. Fragrance can truly be an integral asset for anxiety-alleviation (in addition to other things!).

5. The Art Of Touch

Give every youngster an article to contact, for example, a ball, a plume, a delicate toy, a stone, and so on. Request that they close their eyes and portray what the article feels like to an accomplice. At that point, have the accomplices' exchange places. Both this exercise and the past one are basic, yet convincing approaches to show the kids the act of segregating their faculties from each other and tuning into particular encounters.

6. The Heartbeat Exercise

Have the kids bounce around set up for one moment. At that point, have them sit down and place their hands on their souls. Guide them to close their eyes and feel their pulses, their breath, and see what else they notice about their bodies.

7. Heart-To-Heart

Right now, which means that "heart" is less exacting. As it were, this movement could likewise just be classified "We should discuss emotions." So plunk down and coolly, serenely request that the children enlighten you regarding their sentiments. What sentiments do they feel? How would they realize they are feeling those sentiments? Ask them which emotions they like the best.

At that point, ask them what they can improve when they aren't feeling the emotions they like best. Advise them that they can generally work on transforming their considerations into bubbles in the event that they are vexed, they can do the Squish and Relax Meditation in the event that they have to quiet down, and they can take a couple of moments to tune in to their breath or feel their pulses in the event that they need to unwind.

BREATHING EXERCISES

Fun Breathing Exercises For Children

Breathing exercises for children are as valuable as they are helpful. In addition to the fact that they help children to control their feelings better, they improve their capacity to focus, center, and also rest faster. Breathing exercises additionally help children to feel increasingly loose in light of the fact that they can comprehend their body better, and they can even assist improve their elocution and method for imparting.

From the outset, this may appear to be fairly senseless to a few. Don't children show up on the planet, definitely realizing how to relax? Obviously, they do. The biomechanics of breathing in and breathing out are programmed forms that we as a whole do and that nobody has ever needed to instruct us. Notwithstanding, the inquiry that should lead us to a straightforward reflection would we say we are: all expertise to inhale, in any case, do we do it well?

"Breathing exercises advance children's mental health to improve their fixation and lessen the impacts of stress."

We don't generally take in the correct manner. To begin with, a more than evident truth is that we don't utilize our entire lung limit, and we overlook that we likewise have a stomach that can sublimely advance this entire procedure. Additionally, another reality that we mustn't overlook is that when all is said in done, we inhale rapidly; we take in little air with each breath in, and this causes us to inhale all the more frequently and out of beat.

This converts into tiredness, visits cerebral pains, and the effect of stress and anxiety on the body. Moreover, corresponding to babies, there is another inquisitive truth to consider. At the point when a kid shows up on the planet, they inhale effectively – profoundly and utilizing the stomach. Nonetheless, as they develop, regardless of whether because of stance or way of life, they bit by bit lose this common capacity.

Hence, utilizing games to show children how to inhale "well" will empower them to recuperate this overlooked capacity, thus improve their personal satisfaction.

Breathing exercises for children

This exercise reinforced the mind circuits of the children to improve their procedures of fixation and passionate administration. The children who had just gone through over 2 years rehearsing these early daytime breathing meetings indicated fewer consideration issues and less hyperactivity just as more prominent eagerness to contemplate and learn.

As should be obvious, something as straightforward and fundamental as devoting a little break in the day to this arrangement of breathing exercises can emphatically effect on children's advancement and capacities. It merits attempting. We should view a portion of the systems:

1. The snake game

Straightforward, fun, and viable. The snake game is a most loved among little children and comprises of the accompanying:

- Have the children sitting in seats and guide them to sit back straight.

- Instruct them to put their hands on their mid-region and spotlight on the guidelines they will hear.

- •

- Then, they have to take in profoundly through the nose for 4 seconds (you can check the time for them), seeing how their midsections swell.

- •

- Afterward, they have to let out the air by making the sound of a snake, a noisy murmur that should keep going as long as they can.

2. Exploding a major inflatable

The second exercise for children is similarly fun. It comprises of the accompanying advances:

- The youngster ought to sit easily on a seat with their back straight.

- Now you disclose to them that the game comprises of exploding an imperceptible inflatable, a brilliant inflatable that necessities to get incredibly huge.

- To do this, they have to take in through the nose and afterward inhale out, envisioning how the inflatable is growing up and getting greater and greater.

Right now, it will, in general, take in through the mouth. Indeed, this is the thing that we as a whole do when we explode an inflatable. In this way, you have to address them and guide them to take in through the nose as their stomachs swell up, and afterward breathe out puckering their lips as though they were exploding that immense beautiful inflatable.

3. Breathing game

Breathing game is one of the exercise, which most triumphs among little children. They truly love it. This is your main thing:

- The children ought to be on their feet with their legs marginally separated.

- Tell them that they will become elephants and inhale like them.

- They need to take in profoundly through the nose and, as they do as such, lift their arms up as though they were the elephant's trunk, attempting to make their stomaches swell simultaneously.

- Then to breathe out, they have to inhale out noisily through the mouth and bring their arms down as they twist down a bit of, bringing the "elephant trunk" down.

4. Panther breathing

The remainder of these breathing exercises for children is more muddled; however, similarly fun and compelling for getting them to inhale with the stomach.

- Instruct the children to get down on the floor down on the ground as though they were a panther.

- Then they have to take in through the nose, seeing how their stomach expands up and their spinal segment goes down.

- Now they ought to inhale out through the mouth and perceive how their paunch discharges and their back ascents up a piece.

These exercises ought to be done gradually with the goal that the children notice these procedures in the children body and can relate them to this sort of breathing, which, generally, is the most useful.

Taking everything into account, there are a lot of all the more breathing exercises for children. It's a smart thought to discover those which they like best and which they can do all the means of appropriately, and afterward make them part of their day by day schedule. Just along these lines will they figure out how to inhale better, thus reinforce their improvement and their personal satisfaction.

Recorded here are other ten of the simplest, generally fun and best breathing exercises for kids.

1. Blossom Breaths:

Aroma and shade of blossoms frequently draw in kids. So encourage kids to bloom breathing exercises. Give your child a fragrant, brilliant bloom, and instruct him to take in through the nose and inhale out through the mouth. Bloom breaths help discharge pressure. Offer your child blossoms like daffodils, daisies, and roses.

2. Murmuring Breaths:

Murmuring breaths assist kids with interfacing with their internal identity and loosen up them genuinely and intellectually. Show your child to take in through the nose. Cause him to breathe in a full breath, and afterward request that he breathe out through the mouth while making a murmuring sound like a snake. Dragging out the exhalation will enable your child to unwind and feel much improved.

3. Bear Breaths:

Bear breaths help your child feel intelligent and loosen up his psyche and body. Advise your kid to envision a bear resting. Instruct him to breathe in air through nose and respite and check three, two, and one and breathe out again before tallying three, two, and one. Rehash it five times. Your child will feel loose and without stress.

4. Elephant Breaths:

Elephant breathing exercises assist wake with increasing your drowsy kid. Get him to remain with his feet wide separated. Instruct him to dangle his arms in front like an elephant trunk. At that point, guide him to take in through the nose and raise his arms high over his head. Instruct him to inhale out through the mouth, swinging the arms down. Rehash the breathing exercise three times. Your child will feel vigorous.

5. Rabbit Breaths:

This is one of the intriguing breathing procedures for kids. Kids love rabbits. During rabbit breathing exercises, kids profess to be little rabbits and sniff like rabbits. Encourage your child to do three fast sniffs through the nose and afterward breathe out one full breath through the nose. Rabbit breaths help quiet your irritated child and assist him with breathing easily with no breathing trouble.

6. Air pocket Bee Breaths:

Air pocket Bee breaths are additionally well known as Bhramari in Pranayama methods and assist kids with controlling their breaths successfully. Cause your child to sit easily with crossed legs. Request that he closes his eyes. Guide him to take in through the nose, with the fingers in the ears, and inhale out, making the sound of a murmuring honey bee. Reverberation happening during the breath offers your child a quieting impact as well as causes him to have solid eyes.

7. Sight-seeing Balloon Breaths:

Sight-seeing balloon breathing exercise offers your child a loosening up impact and lifts his creative mind. Cause your child to sit in with folded legs position easily and cup hands around the mouth. Guide him to breathe in air profoundly through the nose and breathe out through the mouth while tossing his hands outwards as though your child is blowing a gigantic sight-seeing balloon. At the point when he breathes out the air totally, instruct him to take in gradually appreciating the large inflatable influencing noticeable all around.

8. Tummy Breathing:

Tummy breathing drives away your child's miserable state of mind and encourages him to feel sans stress. Advise your child to lie on his back, shutting his eyes and with his hands on the tummy.

Instruct him to unwind and afterward breathe in gradually through the nose with a shut mouth. Hold the breath for five seconds and gradually inhale out.

9. Chakra Breathing:

This is one of the powerful, profound breathing exercises for children. Chakra breathing empowers seven chakras present in a body. Advise your child to stand up standing with his feet wide, separated, and inhale fast. Keep the mouth open all through the breathing procedure. Encourage your child to concentrate on his breathing as it assists with invigorating seven chakras.

10. Gyan Mudra Breathing:

Gyan Mudra breathing loosens up your little one and improves his fixation. Cause your child to sit straight on the ground. Spot the wrists on the knees and make him join the tips of forefinger and thumb to make 'Gyan Mudra.' Close the eyes. Show the child to breathe regularly, center around the breath as he breathes in, and breathes out the air through the nostrils.

RELAXING EXERCISES

This sort of issue with nodding off is typical for some kids, yet it's not the same as a crying infant or the little child who pitches a temper fit. "Rest preparing" takes on new importance at this stage and turns into more about mental preparation.

The uplifting news is there are straightforward systems you can utilize and educate, which can enable your kids to get past the night with negligible shouting, crying, or dissatisfaction.

The methodologies I draw on originate from my own preparation and practice in careful meditation. While further developed quiet meditation meetings are suitable and extraordinarily helpful for guardians, kids profit by shorter, more straightforward, guided mindfulness exercises.

Insight: before you begin, consider conversing with your youngster about how the cerebrum functions utilizing these accommodating tips from Mindful.org.

For every one of the bedtime exercises underneath, I urge you to have your kid start by taking three to five careful breaths, in through the nose and out through the mouth ("smell the blossoms, victory the candles"). Urge them to attempt to hinder a tad with every breath.

At the point when they are quieted and prepared, have them attempt one of the accompanying exercises, introduced arranged by effortlessness and as a content that you can use to mentor your youngster:

1 COUNTING YOUR BREATHS

Presently, as you take in and out, I need you to begin gradually tallying your breath. Take in – "1" – inhale out "2" – take in "3" – inhale out "4" – and continue tallying until you find a workable pace. At that point, begin once more at one. In the event that you forget about where you are, don't stress over it by any stretch of the imagination. Simply start back at 1 and prop up until you feel tired and nod off.

2 BODY SCAN

Presently we're going to help each piece of your body to unwind and nod off. Close your eyes, and simply tune in to my words as I manage you through it. Try not to stress if you get diverted. At the point when you notice you're contemplating something different, simply center back in around my voice and listen once more.

We'll begin with your toes. Squirm your toes around a tad and afterward let them unwind. Your toes are feeling extremely sluggish and extremely overwhelming. Inhale into your toes, and when you breathe out, let them unwind significantly more. Presently let that casual inclination move into your feet, through your impact point, and up to your lower leg. Presently your feet are completely loose and tired.

Go through this equivalent content to travel through your kid's body right to the head. Make certain to talk gradually and tranquility, and step by step, decline your voice to a murmur.

3 GUIDED IMAGERY

How about we attempt to consider something you truly love doing. When you've thought of it, disclose to me a smidgen about it. For instance, I realize you truly love skiing. Will we consider your preferred path at your preferred mountain?

Use models that are fitting to your kid. When they have recognized something they love doing, start inciting them to thoroughly consider that experience from start to finish, focusing on what they see, hear, feel, or in any case, sense as they travel through the experience.

One of the advantages of doing these exercises with your youngster is that you are instructing them to know about how their cerebrum functions and how they can deal with their "monkey mind." This kind of information is transferable to a wide range of circumstances and honestly serves grown-ups the same amount as it serves kids.

Unwinding contents for kids are a lot of equivalent to unwinding for grown-ups, depending on basic unwinding strategies. These contents are compelling for the individuals who are new in learning to unwind or for the individuals who appreciate brief and straightforward unwinding methods. They and can be utilized as a speedy technique for unwinding for kids or grown-ups.

These free unwinding contents can be utilized to figure out how to unwind or record your own unwinding sound CD. Figure out how to unwind or discover your unwinding style with these contents.

Here are some free unwinding contents for kids:

Unwinding for Children Relaxation for children that guide children or grown-ups to loosen up utilizing basic breathing and dynamic unwinding methods. This content is proposed to be utilized with the direction of a grown-up.

Breathing Relaxation for Children This breathing unwinding for children is for any individual who is figuring out how to unwind. The two children and grown-ups can utilize this breathing unwinding exercise as a simple unwinding method.

Unwinding to Stop Being Afraid of the Dark This unwinding content is for children or grown-ups who fear the dim. It starts with perception and quieting expressions to bring solace and unwinding, and finishes with aloof dynamic muscle unwinding. Tune in to this unwinding content before bed to nod off easily.

Guided Imagery for Writing an Exam This guided symbolism content will permit you to envision the way toward reading for and composing a test. Picturing achievement will advance expanded certainty, fixation, and memory. Unwinding can likewise improve the capacity to learn by dispensing with a portion of the anxiety that meddles with taking in new data.

Unwinding to Decrease Fidgeting This unwinding content will assist you with decreasing squirming with your hands. This exercise will permit you to lessen anxiety to make a sentiment of quiet stay composed, in any event, when confronted with stress.

VISUALIZATION EXERCISES FOR KIDS

Representation Exercises

1) To show that to the psyche, a genuine and an envisioned occasion is the equivalent, request that your kid imagine he is holding a large portion of a lemon. Feel it in your grasp; imagine you can see it. Press it and feel the wetness of the juice streaming over your hand. Presently bring that lemon up to your mouth and guzzle up a significant piece of juice – watch your youngster's face as he does this, and you're ensured a decent chuckle! Presently ask him, what does it suggest a flavor like? Did you get an acrid preference for your mouth?

2) Close your eyes and envision two mutts playing. Get your youngster to time you, and do this for 1 moment. Open your eyes and compose a rundown of things to depict what you saw. Presently request that your youngster close his eyes and envision two canines playing. Time him and request that he open his eyes following a moment and rundown everything about what he saw. The champ is the individual with the greatest rundown!

3) Sit down with your youngster and conceptualize different positive expresses that he should stay, for instance, focusing, concentrating effectively, and being empowered. Essentially the mindfulness that he can utilize his brain and body to get to these states when he needs to, instead of simply hanging tight for them to sneak up on him, is a major advance. In the event that you additionally urge him to make his own arrangement of grapples to use again and again to make positive states in himself, you will have given him an incredible blessing that will profit him for an amazing remainder.

DREAMY VISUALIZATION FOR KIDS

Inventive Visualization for Children-A Childhood Gift

In contrast to us, kids are not very worried about future occasions. Quickly, they may get agitated when they don't get what they need at the same time, they tend to forget about it effectively, and that is the reason I would like accentuation that imaginative representation for children ought to be an unscripted procedure.

Kids are normally talented with the inventive capacity; we as a whole were incredible in utilizing our creative mind to make the fantasy environment for our playtime. On the off chance that you will take a live case of any gathering of kids playing, you will find that there is many inventive components being joined in their games.

The vast majority of us neglect to make the most of our fantasy world as we grow up in light of the fact that our general public doesn't energize such propensities.

Today, perception is one of the most urgent mind devices accessible to us anyway the basic characteristics expected to utilize it is something we have to secure with training.

All things considered, it's anything but a learning procedure, be that as it may, an unlearning procedure.

The facts demonstrate that we can't take care of what has befallen us previously in any case. We can, without a doubt, help the youthful ones of our age.

It Should Be Fun

The slip-up a great many people make is that they attempt to instruct kids to envision in the procedure they have figured out how to do it rather, we ought to be the ones gaining from them.

No kid will consent to sit like you and envision their wants getting satisfied; in the event that you will constrain them, at that point, they will deceive you like in different cases.

What we neglect to see is that our longing isn't their craving, and it just can never be, you can convince them to adhere to your guidelines, yet you can't produce the energy that is required to accomplish any objective.

No psyche instrument can work in the event that it doesn't create the enthusiasm of the person. It ought to be an enjoyment procedure.

You might need to make the youngster a virtuoso at the same time. The kid is absolutely ignorant of what a "virtuoso" is and why the damnation is it important to be one?

Thus, encouraging kids to imagine your direction is certifiable, not a smart thought.

How to Make It Interesting?

'On the off chance that you need to show children how to imagine, at that point, you will initially need to drop all "your vision" for them and with a receptive outlook acknowledge their fantasies as yours.

Their longing could be as little like from figuring out how to ride a bike to as large as turning into the best footballer of the world. You ought not to pass judgment on it.

Keep in mind. It is we grown-ups who are excessively connected to the results, that is the reason we don't set out to think something important.

In all actuality right now, we can envision anything we desire and appreciate the inclination without being worried about the final products at the same time. You can't envision being the best footballer in the world, right?... Kids can!

It's just plain obvious. We truly don't need to show them how to envision yet there two things we could accomplish for their self-awareness:-

1-Motivate them to utilize their imaginative capacity.

2-Give their fantasies a legitimate heading since they won't have the option to get clear about their dreams until you ask them a couple of inquiries about their fantasies.

dream

COLLECTION OF MEDITATION STORIES FOR KIDS OF 5/10 YEARS OLD.

IN THE FAIRY CASTLE

ONCE UPON A NIGHT...
There were two children named Kate and Harry. They had a radiant nursery, and they wanted to play in it.

One radiant, Spring day, Kate's blue hair strip left her hair while she was playing in the nursery with Harry. The breeze blew it down a little way. Kate pursued it, with Harry following her. They ran down the way for quite a while, pursuing the little strip. At last, it halted. Kate got it and glanced around. "Harry," she stated, "I don't accept we've been right now the nursery previously." "Neither have I," answered Harry. He peered toward a little bush. It was somewhat shining. A gleaming fog emerged from its branches. He wandered into it. At that point out of nowhere, he halted. He was unable to accept what he saw "Hello! Kate," he cried, "I state, I've discovered a little château!"

Kate came running. She panted when she saw the manor. It was making the bush gleam and sparkle as it did, for it shimmered like silver.

In the meantime, inside the château, a little fairy princess named Jessica was disturbed. She had been startled by Harry's enormous holler, and she had covered up in the most distant corner of a turret. At that point, a major eye showed up in the window. It was Kate's eye. Jessica let out a screech. Kate removed her eye from the window. "There's a fairy in there!" she cried.

Harry rushed to the window and peeped in. Jessica, requiring some barrier, tossed her little pack of enchantment fairy dust at Harry. Promptly, they shrank down to fairy-size.

Kate looked down at herself in wonder. At that point, without speculation, she hurried to the little mansion entryway and thumped on it. Jessica replied. She took a gander at Kate in anxiety. "Leave! You alarm me," she said fearlessly. Kate grinned, it was a benevolent grin. "I won't hurt you," she said. Her voice was relieving to the point that Jessica really wanted to give her access. Harry came in also.

Jessica gave them some chocolate buns and some velvety milk. They had a fine evening. Tragically, however, it was before a long time to leave, so Kate and Harry set on their way home.

Jessica, the Fairy Princess, is an awesome companion of the children now. However, their fellowship is a mystery, for nobody could ever trust Kate and Harry on the off chance that they said they were companions with a fairy!!!

GOOD NIGHT.......

THE THREE TASKS

Lily stood sobbing close to the timberland. It was past 12 PM and black as night. She felt appallingly terrified. Her mistress got her a vehicle and dropped her close to the timberland and left.

It was her discipline for copying a gap in her mistress' dress incidentally while pressing. Lily shuddered. Lily could likewise hear the thunder of a lion out there. She shut her eyes and supplicated. Unexpectedly a hand on her shoulder made her open her eyes. Lily observed an old woman conveying a stick remaining before her.

"For what reason do you pain, kid?" the elderly person inquired. The young lady related her life's story. That she was a vagrant just ten years of age, having lost both her folks in a fender bender. She functioned as a servant in a house, where she was routinely reviled and mishandled by her lord and mistress. Lily took a breather. Her eyes blurred as she told the old woman that she had a senior sister, sixteen years of age, who went into the forested areas two years back to gather wood and stayed away forever.
The old woman inquired. Lily gestured, barely accepting what she had simply heard. The old woman drove her profound into the backwoods, and there, directly in the center of the wood, Lily observed a cabin with a light consuming inside. A hot bowl of soup was sitting tight for her on the table. The woman likewise gave Lily some comfortable garments to wear.

The next morning after breakfast, which comprised of porridge, the old woman addressed Lily. "You can remain here for all time, yet before that, you need to finish three undertakings that I dispense you." She put a pitcher in Lily's grasp. "Bring me water from the cascade, yet recollect a drop shouldn't spill." As Lily was conveying the pitcher, it tumbled from her hand and split. Lily was in tears. What was she to do? Woody, the woodpecker, who had been observing Lily with the pitcher in her grasp, traveled to the kikar tree and, utilizing his sharp nose, brought gum from the tree for Lily. The split was fixed, and Lily had the option to convey water in the pitcher. The old woman was satisfied.

Following day the woman gave Lily a lit light. "Get me some basil leaves to make tea. However, recall, there must be light in the light." Lily gathered some basil leaves and put them in the bin the woman had given her yet while restoring a solid breeze put out the light in the light. Contemplations of a perpetual home subsided from Lily's psyche when abruptly twelve sparkle worms settled themselves on the lamp. The old woman snickered with fulfillment when she saw the scene.

The next morning Lily needed to play out the last errand. The old woman put her pet hare in her arms. "Put a band around her neck; however, recall it ought not to be fake and not felt with one's fingers." Lily didn't have the foggiest idea what to do, on the off chance that she utilized blossoms that would handily be felt. She drew close to the hibiscus plant. "Press us and let the juice structure a characteristic band on the rabbit's neck," the blossoms entreated her. The rabbit presently had a red band around her neck.

As Lily returned, she saw a major house remaining instead of the hovel. The woods had vanished, and there was a street driving towards the town. What astounded Lily and filled her with happiness was her sister sitting on the bed, hanging tight for her.

"I was in imprisonment for a long time helpless before a devilish old witch who treated me like a slave," her sister Rita said. "In any case, where was the old woman?" Lily checked out her.

"Have you seen a fairy godmother here?" Her sister shook her head. Lily understood that the fairy godmother had the option to break the devilish witch's revile and had liberated her sister.'

"Much obliged to you fairy back up parent do come and see me soon," Lily murmured in her rest, as the two sisters went to bed with a wonderful first light anticipating them.

They would go to class once more. Develop vegetables in the garden and gain their work and live joyfully ever after.

GOOD NIGHT ....

KNIGHT AND PERSIE

A while back, Persie was the sun, and Knight was an inquisitive man.

Knight saw Persie sparkling as splendidly as precious stones ablaze in the sky. He was in the stunningness of her warm sparkle and loved her from Earth. She was splendid to such an extent that it hurt his eyes to view her legitimately. Persie adored Knight too. She saw the exertion he made to appreciate her and wanted for him to be near her. He would never take a gander at her nor go after her without being in incredible agony! She was so splendid! It made Persie tragic to realize her gleam was agonizing to her Knight. However, she was the sun. She gave Earth warmth and light. It was in her temperament to sparkle, and there was no other path for her to be less sun. Their affection was awful yet evident. The two of them wanted for something very similar to hold one another and love together forever, yet they couldn't as it caused them both extraordinary distress.

Knight was shrewd. He chose to make a defensive layer made of his dedication to Persie to shield himself from her compelling fire. He figured, "That I may securely connect with Persie without being singed to debris nor blinded by her great touch. " Surely, this material would withstand her incredible being, and they could be as one at long last. Persie watched Knight drudge tirelessly over the protective layer.

Finally, he came to Persie after his lovely, shining, protective layer was created. She enthusiastically contacted him; however, she softened his protective layer in one minute! "God help us!" she shouted. She hadn't intended! Knight was shocked and baffled that his protection was so effortlessly pulverized, yet he, despite everything, worshiped her. Notwithstanding, Persie was likewise vexed that her touch had caused him so much distress. Their affection was heartbreaking yet evident. The two of them wanted something very similar, to hold and love each other forever. Yet, they couldn't be as one as it caused them both inconvenience.

Regardless of Knight, he utilized his gigantic heart to form himself a shroud made of his affection for Persie. It was the most grounded material at any point made in the entirety of time! Doubtlessly, this time, the shroud would withstand her forceful touch, and they could at long last be as one.

Knight, at that point, secured himself with the shroud and went to Persie again. He was a man in affection, resolved to hold Persie near him. At the point when she saw him in the shroud, she was overwhelmed with satisfaction and shone more brilliant than any time in recent memory. This made Knight anxious. The shroud was sensitive. He was uncertain in the event that it would be pulverized by her serious beams. He contacted her in any case. At that point, something enchanted occurred! They had the option to at long last hold one another! Knight gave her joy, and she wished to restore that satisfaction to him. The shroud permitted them to be close! She inquired as to whether he might want to turn into a Moon. He blissfully acknowledged!

For quite a while, they remained nearby to one another. However, his light failed to measure up to her wondrous gleam. At the point when he turned into the moon, the creatures of Earth were in stunningness of him. Knight was thoughtful, and he adored Persie without a doubt, so he could never request that her sparkle short of what him. He inquired as to whether she might want to take a stab at his shroud. Persie was enchanted that he would offer his beautiful shroud to be folded over her divine body, she concurred. When Persie put on the shroud, something stunning occurred! The space around her was promptly hung with dimness. Neither of them anticipated that! However, the creatures of Earth experienced passionate feelings for Knight! What's more, they started to sing and acclaim him as they had applauded Persie. When Persie saw this, she cherished Knight considerably more, on the off chance that it was conceivable! They remained along these lines for quite a while.

Notwithstanding, the Earth was becoming ill without Does warmth and light. She made Knight mindful of this, and he got tragic, on the grounds that he realized his pale light was insufficient in contrast with the blessing her splendor gave the Earth. Knight was canny. He realized that without the Earth, he would receive no applause from the creatures who lived there. He had sympathy for them as he was previously a human himself.

So Knight and Persie made a guarantee together. Persie would wear Knight's shroud for a brief timeframe with the goal that the two of them could sparkle in their own specific manner for the individuals who cherished them most. Persie and Knight love each other so much. They alternate wearing Knight's shroud made of his unadulterated love for her. Persie sparkles consistently, and Knight is in every case near her demonstrating his dedication and love. Similarly, as they had needed from the start. No more did they endure. Their adoration is valid, however, no longer appalling.

THE LION AND A MOUSE

One day a mouse was looking for nourishment in the backwoods. While looking through, it drew close to the lair of a lion and smelled something wonderful. The mouse ate many pieces. Seeing the numerous pieces that are left over yonder, it has chosen to remain on with the goal that it can eat it in the night moreover. Having eaten such a lot of meat, it was fast sleeping in practically no time.

It has gotten dull, and the Lion came back to its nook. Since it was dim, it couldn't see the mouse dozing on the floor. The Lion had carried with it a bit of a sheep and ate it completely, leaving the bones aside.

The Lion, after some time, had worked off and begun wheezing uproariously. The lion's wheezing woke up the mouse. The mouse ran willy nilly and knock on the lion's leg. The mouse felt the hide on the leg smooth and began investigating it. As it arrived at the ear of the lion, the lion got disturbed and woke up with an unexpected yank that made the mouse descend. Who is here? – the lion thundered. The little mouse with a weak voice answered, " I am a mouse here." How could you upset my rest, and where right? – again yelled the lion.
I am heartbroken, and I am here – said the mouse. The Lion lit a light and looked for the mouse. It found the sanctum clean without any bits of meat and bones; lastly, it saw a mouse in an edge

of its lair shuddering with dread. The mouse looked lovely. The lion thought for some time. It believed that since the mouse was here, its sanctum is kept clean else. It would be smelling with meat pieces and bones all around. Why not permit this mouse to be here, so it keeps the lair clean by consuming the bones and extra meat – therefore the lion pondered.

Alright, reveal to me for what reason did to enter my nook? – The lion proceeded with its inquiry.

The mouse answered with collapsed hands: I was looking for nourishment. I am grieved, I will leave currently if it's not too much trouble permit me to go".

Alright, if you need to remain here, you can do as such, yet you will not upset my rest.

The dread of the mouse didn't diminish. So it has rehashed:" Please permit me to go."

Seeing the mouse in that dreadful condition, the lion felt frustrated about it and said in an extremely delicate tone: Oh little mouse, don't get startled. Simply hear me out cautiously. I chase regular and bring the remains of some creature. I don't eat it completely. You are a little creature, and henceforth, you can without much of a stretch eat the remains and be upbeat. In the event that you like eating like this without looking for nourishment, you can remain here.

The mouse was astonished, and with joy, it said, " Yes, Mr. Lion, I will remain in the sanctum" One more condition: Said the lion.

You should keep the cave clean by eating all the extra bits of meat and bones. In the event that you can not eat completely, you will divert them and keep the nook clean.

Alright, Mr. Lion said the mouse.

Alright now, you rest in that corner, and I will rest here in the center of the cave: saying this, the lion rested.

The mouse has a propensity for moving uninhibitedly on the floor while dozing. Along these lines, by 12 PM, the mouse came closer to the lion and began feeling its glow and dove further deep into the rest. In the rest, it began soothing itself by setting itself in the overlay of the lion's leg.

The lion additionally felt it OK and adjusted its leg to allow the mouse to rest.

The lion watched the mouse for quite a while, and later, it woke up the mouse carefully with its paw. It cried uproariously and endeavored to jump out, notwithstanding, hindered carefully by the lion.

Do be alarmed, you have laid on my leg, and along these lines, I woke you up from sleep: said the lion. The mouse broke into portions of chuckling. Seeing mouse, the lion too much started laughing.

Together the lion and the mouse lived always....

LENNY THE FLYING INVENTOR

Quite a long time ago, there was a clever person named Lenny. Lenny was an innovator. He created a wide range of contraptions. His home resembled a wreck, yet he had some truly cool things.

One day Lenny chose he needed to fly.

"I will create a few wings and fly," Lenny told his companion Rudy.

"Presently, I really know you've gone crazy. Nobody saw Lenny for quite a long time. At that point, one day, he left his workshop with an extraordinary huge smile all over.

He called Rudy on the telephone. "Rudy, tomorrow I will fly, yet I need your assistance," said Lenny.

"Did you truly manufacture a few wings?" asked Rudy.

"No doubt, and they are extremely delightful," said Lenny. "They're somewhat overwhelming, however.
"Metal! Wouldn't you say that it will be too overwhelming to even think about using for wings?" asked Rudy.

"No, I determined the entirety of the points. I will resemble a human plane," said Lenny.

Rudy simply feigned exacerbation. "Alright, I will be over before anything else, and we'll give them a shot," said Rudy.

"See you at that point," said Lenny.

The following morning they hauled the wings up to the highest point of Kill Devil Hill, and Lenny tied them on.

"Is it proper to say that you are certain those are not very substantial? Asked Rudy once more.

"No, matter how faster I run, the lighter they will get. The breeze will lift me up, and I will be flying," said Lenny, unquestionably.

"Good, I will get a running beginning and take off," said Lenny. In this way, Lenny upheld up around fifty feet and began running. As he ran, the heaviness of the wings began to destroy his legs, and he got lower and lower to the ground. Similarly, as he found a good pace of the slope, his legs gave out, and he slid over the ground all over.

After Rudy moved around on the ground, chuckling for about a moment, he found a good pace, Lenny, on the off chance that he was Ok.

"No doubt, Yeah, genuinely interesting," said Lenny. "I surmise you might be correct. They are somewhat overwhelming, yet I realize the shape is perfect. I will simply return to the workshop and make them out of another material. Something lighter"

Two or after three weeks, Lenny called up Rudy.

"I've done it," said Lenny.

"You've done what?" asked Rudy.

"I made the wings.
"I'm in transit," said Rudy.

At the point when Rudy showed up, Lenny was up on the rooftop with these amusing looking pink wings.

"Pink wings!" giggled Rudy.

"Better believe it, this is the stuff I had leftover from when I created that mammoth Pig robot we utilized on Halloween a year ago," said Lenny.

"Do you believe you're simply going to bounce off and fly?" asked Rudy.

"Better believe it. Here goes," said Lenny.

He sponsored up a little and took a snappy scramble and a bounce.

Aaaaaaaaaaagh, SMACK! The wings severed right, and Lenny arrived on his head in certain brambles alongside the house.

After Rudy moved around on the ground giggling for about a moment, he found a workable pace, Lenny, on the off chance that he was Ok.

"Better believe it, Yeah, genuinely clever," said Lenny. "I surmise they may have been somewhat frail, yet I realize the shape is perfect. I will simply return to the workshop and make them out of another material. Something not as substantial as the piece metal and not as light as the tissue paper."

"Sounds like a smart thought to me," said Rudy as he feigned exacerbation.

Half a month later, Lenny called up Rudy.

"I've truly done it this time," said Lenny.

"You've done what?" asked Rudy.

"I modified the wings with wax and balsa wood. These things look simply like feathered creature's wings. Meet me at Kill Devil Hill. I need an observer," said Lenny.

"I'm in transit," said Rudy.

At the point when Rudy showed up, he saw the wings. They looked great!

"I need you to assist me with tying them on," said Lenny.

Rudy helped him tie on the wings. They fit genuinely cozy. There was a handle under each wing out close to the tip for Lenny to use to move the wings here and there and a belt that circumvented his waste with the goal that they would not tumble off.

"Here we go," hollered Lenny as he sponsored up and started running towards the peak of the slope.

He didn't back off, and similarly, as he found a workable pace of the slope, he began to lift very high. He was flying!

YAHOOO! Hollered Lenny. He flew and flew simply snickering and hooting. He flew ever more elevated. He was truly getting high now, and he began to stress. "How would I land these things?" he asked himself.

That question was going to be replied. Out of nowhere, he saw that his wings were beginning to dissolve. He had ascended so high, that the sun was beginning to liquefy the wax he used to make the wings. Truly soon, he had infinitesimal wings, and he was flying around a hundred miles an hour down towards the forested areas.

"Kid, this is going harmed once more," said Lenny to himself.

He collided with the trees.

Rudy ran up, "Are all of you, right?" he inquired.

"Better believe it, I suspect as much, yet I am certainly going to stop attempting to fly. This is excessively unpleasant on the body," said Lenny.

Right up 'til the present time, nobody trusts Rudy when he recounts to the story of how Lenny flew like a winged animal. It might be acceptable that they don't trust him since others would presumably get injured, as did Lenny.

Lenny additionally made a responsibility not to concoct whatever can't be utilized while standing immovably on the ground.

He regularly tells individuals, "If individuals were intended to fly, they would have wings!"

The end.

BRITNEY THE HAMSTER

There was a savvy little hamster named Britney. He lived in a butcher shop claimed by a man named Mr. Luiz. Mr. Luiz didn't give a lot of consideration to Brithney. Brithney had no enclosure – he went anyplace in the shop he satisfied. Mr. Luiz would put out some bread scraps for Brithney once in a while. Be that as it may, generally, Brithney was all alone, scrambling around searching for nourishment and water.

Brithney was forlorn living this way. He simply needed to be somebody's pet – to live in a comfortable enclosure with shavings to make a home, and heaps of good crunchy nourishment. Brithney was worn out on being ravenous, and he needed to be cherished!

So consistently, when Brithney heard the chimes jingle on the shop entryway, he realized a client would stroll in and take a gander at the meats. Brithney would scramble on the wooden containers, and holler "Hello, Mister! I'd make an extraordinary pet! Will you take me home? Hello, look! I can do stunts. What about 'a reverse somersault!" Then Brithney would bounce out of sight and do a retrogressive somersault.

Sadly, however, clients simply didn't see Brithney. What's more, to a human, Brithney's shouting just seemed like "eeeeeh, eeeeeh."
At some point, in the same way as other different days, a man remained outside the shop perusing the store signs. Brithney had perused the signs, as well, and was watching the man. The man came in, took a gander at Mr. Luiz, and stated, "Where's the hamburger?" And Brithney, who was exceptionally eager at this point, said, "Hello! Where's the grain?!" But obviously, he just seemed like "eeeeeh." Brithney knew at this point he needed to plan something extraordinary to forget consideration. So he chose to make a major sign, as well.

Brithney saw a major purple pen, and he discovered some banner paper scraps. He grabbed the pen, which obviously is long to a hamster, and composed on the banner paper, "My name is Brithney, it would be ideal if you take me home to be your pet." Then Brithney waved the sign all around noticeable all around.

The man realized that most hamsters couldn't peruse or compose and believed this must be a stunt. So he said to Mr. Luiz, the butcher, "Luiz, you should be attempting to dispose of your pet hamster." Mr. Luiz stated, "Nah, the little person just hangs around here."

Brithney realized this was his opportunity to be somebody's pet. So he then grabbed the pen, turned the banner paper over, and was going to compose another message.

The man gazed at Brithney, thinking the Hamster had bitten on the pen, and he said, "What a wreck!" Thinking rapidly, Brithney composed on the sign, "Pets Are Purple, Too!"

Furthermore, as the man understood this hamster could really peruse and compose, he started to get a thought. This little person would make an incredible pet! The kids would cherish him!

With Mr. Luiz's authorization, the man scooped Brithney up, put him in a decent box, then take him to a pet store where he purchased all the extravagant little gear hamsters should be upbeat. At home, his kids wiped off all the purple ink and gave Brithney a small little pen and a minuscule little scratchpad. (The principal question they asked Brithney was "What is your name?") From that time on, Brithney lived joyfully ever after with his new family.

UP, UP AND AWAY

Up, Up and Away

Quite a while back, when I was eight, my father took me angling. It was in April, the principal day of the angling season in northern Quebec. What's more, I couldn't have cared less on the off chance that it was cold.

"Assist me with finding my warm boots?" I inquired. Also, he did. At that point, I helped father make nutty spread sandwiches, my top choice. "Where's my packsack?" I inquired. Grinning calmly, he discovered it for me.

"This is the way I will get a fish," I said. Holding my new angling pole birthday present full stretch, I saw its perfect lines, firmly twisted strings, and sparkling eyelets. At that point, swinging it around, smacked the water glass from the kitchen table. The beneficial thing he helped me tidy up all odds and ends.

Mother just stood and shook her head. I don't think she was vexed. Simply happy, her young men were going angling together, anyplace out of the house.

We stacked up against our pickup truck. First, my angling pole bar was excessively long in the front. So I set it in the back. At that point, I put our packsacks with sandwiches and water directly next to it. Nearly overlooked our angling box with some flawless draws, yet father didn't. He gave the green tin box to me.

The rock street was brimming with free stones. What's more, they flew behind us as though discharged from slingshots. Be that as it may, I was unable to see much in light of the residue. At that point, we hit a colossal knock. "My angling pole!" I hollered, as I watched it skip from the truck. Father put the brakes on so hard I flew over the seat and nearly stifled out and about residue that before long secured us.

"I saw it fly over that dump," I said. Father climbed down the roadside. Also, I stepped on some ice. "Try not to get wet!" I hollered. In any case, he did.

Before long, father returned with my perfect blessing, scratched and canvassed in the mud. The wrecked plug handle made it shorter than previously. In the wake of beginning our direction, I could now keep my angling pole in my lap. Furthermore, my tears had halted.

It's difficult to attempt to take care of business when your birthday present attempts to take off like a crow at that point gets broken. In any event, it fits inside the front of the truck. "Does that mean I can't go angling? I inquire.

"No," father replied. "I'm going to show you another approach to angle," he said. "Much the same as my own father demonstrated to me."

"In any event, we're despite everything going angling!" I yelled. Inevitably, my cap passed over. Father halted the truck, and this time I came to assist him with discovering it. I made an effort not to see him conversing with himself.

"Keep it in your lap, under the fishing supply container," he recommended. "This is the place our climbing starts," father said when we at long last halted. The path was loaded with a cold trench. He stated, "Make an effort not to get wet." But I did.

It was fun bouncing on the ice. But when I got through. It resembled a freezing/cascade sprinkling everywhere. The beneficial thing he brought some jeans for me. He should realize me truly well at this point.

At last, we arrive at the lake. It appears as though we strolled most of the way around the globe. The vast majority of the ice is no more. Also, a few ducks are swimming. The water's unreasonably cold for me, however. I simply need to angle.

I observe cautiously as a father shows me my granddad's approach to angle, without an angling rod post.
He finds an overwhelming stone, folds some line over it at that point ties a bunch. After that, he makes a little hover with the remainder of the line in a heap adjacent to his foot. What's more, ties a flawless silver spinner on end. At that point, he makes another bunch keeping it fast to the solid dark line.

Holding around three feet of line before him, he starts to spin. He does that a few times and sends it flying over the water. It sure took off, making an overwhelming sprinkle some separation away. I can hardly wait for my turn.

"Do you need some assistance?" Dad inquired.

"No, I need to do everything without anyone else."

"Did you watch all that I did?" he inquired.

"Indeed," I answer. "What's more, I'm going to toss it more distant than you!" I boasted boisterously. I take my line and fold it over another stone. At that point, I make a hover with the rest close to my feet. What's more, tie my exceptional gold spoon on end I am going to toss.

In the wake of ending up like a baseball player, my first toss goes in reverse and gets on a tree appendage. In any case, the father gets it down for me. I think he tore his jeans. Presently I'm prepared to start whirling once more. To start with, I do one major circle, at that point two, at that point three. Lastly, let go. My spoon, similar to a rocket, goes up and up. The sun makes it sparkle.

A fortunate crow escapes the way. The floppy fledgling may believe it's a truck… no, perhaps a plane that flies. My line flies through the air, past a skimming log what's more, over certain ducks on the water.

It proceeds to go and… Oh, goodness. "Father, I neglected to make a bunch when I folded the line over my stone!"

I recollect some time in the past how he shook his head. Also, grinned. Presently I do as well. I thoroughly consider he's still there on the lake. What's more, he's searching for a lost gold spoon for his son.

The Selfish Giant

Each evening, as they were originating from school, the children used to proceed to play in the Giant's nursery.

It was an enormous flawless nursery, with delicate green grass. To a great extent, over the grass stood delightful blossoms like the stars, and there were 12 trees in the spring-time broke out into sensitive blooms of pink and pearl, and in the pre-winter bore rich organic product. The winged animals sat on the trees and sang so sweetly that the children used to stop their games so as to hear them out. "How cheerful we are here!" they cried to one another.

One day the Giant returned. He had been to visit his companion, the Cornish monster, and had remained with him for a long time. After the 7th years were over, he had said all that he needed to state, for his discussion was constrained, and he resolved to come back to his own palace. At the point when he showed up, he saw the children playing in the nursery.

"What is your mission here?" he cried in a blunt voice, and the children fled.

"My own nursery is my own nursery," said the Giant; "anyone can get that, and I will permit no one to play in it yet myself." So he assembled a high divider surrounding it and set up a notification board saying

TRESPASSERS WILL BE PROSECUTED

He was a narrow-minded Giant.

The poor children now had no place to play. They attempted to play out and about, yet the street was exceptionally dusty and brimming with hard stones, and they didn't care for it. They used to meander around the high divider when their exercises were finished and talk about the wonderful nursery inside. "How glad we were there," they said to one another.

At that point, the Spring came, and everywhere throughout the nation, there were little blooms and little winged animals. Just in the nursery of the Selfish Giant, it was still winter. The flying creatures couldn't have cared less to sing in it as there were no children, and the trees neglected to bloom. When an excellent blossom put its head out from the grass, however when it saw the notification board, it was so upset for the children that it slipped over into the ground once more, and headed out to rest. The main individuals who were satisfied were the Snow and the Frost. "Spring has overlooked this nursery," they cried, "so we will live here all the all year." The Snow concealed the grass with her incredible white shroud, and the Frost painted all the trees silver. At that point, they welcomed the North Wind to remain with them, and he came. He was enveloped by hides, and he thundered the entire day about the nursery and blew the fireplace mugs down. "This is a brilliant self-satisfied," he stated, "we should ask the Hail on a visit." So the Hail came. Consistently for three hours, he shook on the top of the stronghold till he broke the greater part of the records, and afterward, he ran all around the nursery as fast as he could go. He was wearing dim, and his breath resembled ice.

"I can't comprehend why the Spring is so late in coming," said the Selfish Giant, as he sat at the window and watched out at his virus white nursery; "I trust there will be an adjustment in the climate."

In any case, the Spring never came, nor the Summer. The Autumn gave the brilliant organic product to each garden, however to the Giant's nursery, she gave none. "He is excessively childish," she said. So it was consistently Winter there, and the North Wind, and the Hail, and the Frost, and the Snow moved about through the trees.

One morning the Giant was lying conscious in bed when he heard some stunning music. It was extremely just a little linnet singing outside his window, yet it was for such a long time since he had heard a flying creature sing in his nursery that it appeared to him to be the most excellent music on the planet. At that point, the Hail quit moving over his head, and the North Wind stopped thundering, and a delectable scent came to him through the open casement. "I accept the Spring has come finally," said the Giant, and he leaped up and watched out.

What did he see?

He saw a superb sight. Through a little opening in the divider, the children had sneaked in, and they were sitting in the parts of the trees. In each tree that he could see, there was a little kid. What's more, the trees were so happy to have the children back again that they had secured themselves with blooms and were waving their arms tenderly over the children's heads. The flying creatures were flying about and twittering with amusing, and the blossoms were turning upward through the green grass and giggling. It was a flawless scene. Just in one corner, it was still winter. It was the most distant corner of the nursery, and in it was standing a young man. He was little to such an extent that he was unable to reach up to the parts of the tree, and he was meandering surrounding it, crying harshly. Poor people tree was still very secured with ice and day off. The North Wind was blowing and thundering above it. "Move up! Young man," said the Tree, and it bowed its branches down as low as possible, yet the kid was excessively small.

Also, the Giant's heart liquefied as he watched out. "How narrow-minded I have been!" he said; "presently, I know why the Spring would not come here. I will put that poor young man on the highest point of the tree, and afterward, I will thump down the divider, and my nursery will be the children's play area forever and ever." He was actually quite upset about what he had done.

So he crawled ground floor and opened the front entryway delicately, and went out into the nursery. In any case, when the children saw him, they were alarmed to the point that they all fled, and the nursery became winter once more. Just the young man didn't run, for his eyes were so loaded with tears that he didn't see the Giant coming. Furthermore, the Giant took up behind him and took him tenderly in his grasp and put him up into the tree. Also, the tree broke on the double into bloom, and the winged animals came and sang on it, and the young man loosened up his two arms and flung them round the Giant's neck, and kissed him. Furthermore, different children, when they saw that the Giant was not devilish any more, returned running, and with them, came the Spring. "It is your nursery now, little children," said the Giant, and he took an incredible hatchet and thumped down the divider. Furthermore, when the individuals were going to advertise at twelve o'clock, they found the Giant playing with the children in the most lovely nursery they had ever observed.

Throughout the day, they played, and at night they went to the Giant to offer him farewell.

"Be that as it may, where is your little buddy?" he stated: "the kid I put into the tree." The Giant adored him the best since he had kissed him.

"We don't have the foggiest idea," addressed the children; "he has left."

"You should guide him no doubt and come here, to-morrow," said the Giant. In any case, the children said that they didn't have the foggiest idea where he lived, and had never observed him; and the Giant felt pitiful.

Each evening, when school was finished, the children came and played with the Giant. Be that as it may, the young man whom the Giant cherished was gone forever. The Giant was benevolent to all the children, yet he yearned for his first little companion and frequently talked about him. "How I might want to see him!" he used to state.

A long time went over, and the Giant became exceptionally old and weak. He was unable to play about any more, so he sat in an enormous easy chair, and viewed the children at their games, and appreciated his nursery. "I have numerous delightful blossoms," he said; "however, the children are the most excellent blossoms of all."

One winter morning, he watched out of his window as he was dressing. He didn't loathe the Winter now, for he realized that it was just the Spring snoozing and that the blossoms were resting.

Unexpectedly he rubbed his eyes in wonder and looked and looked. It unquestionably was a grand sight. In the most remote corner of the nursery was a tree very secured with dazzling white blooms. Its branches were all brilliant, and natural silver products hung down from them, and underneath it stood the young man he had cherished.

The first floor ran the Giant in incredible bliss, and out into the nursery. He rushed over the grass and drew close to the kid. Also, when he came very close, his face developed red with outrage, and he stated, "Who hath set out to twisted thee?" For on the palms of the youngster's hands were the prints of the two nails, and these prints were on the little feet.

"Who hath set out to wound thee?" cried the Giant; "let me know, that I may take my huge sword and kill him."

"Nay!" addressed the youngster, "yet these are the injuries of Love."

"Who workmanship thou?" said the Giant, and an unusual wonderment fell on him, and he bowed before the little youngster.

Furthermore, the kid blessed the Giant, and said to him, "You let me play once in your nursery, to-day, you will accompany me to my nursery, which is Paradise."

What's more, when the children ran in that evening, they found the Giant lying dead under the tree, all secured with white blooms.

THE PEA BLOSSOM

THERE were once five peas in a single shell; they were green, and the shell was green. Thus they accepted that the entire world must be green likewise, which was an exceptionally characteristic end.

The shell developed, and the peas developed, and as they developed, they masterminded themselves all in succession. It looked gentle and pleasant visible to everyone and dull around evening time, similarly as it should. What's more, the peas, as they stayed there, became greater and greater, and increasingly mindful as they considered, for they felt there must be something for them to do.

"Are we to stay here always?" asked one. "Will, we have not become hard, holding up here so long? It appears to me there must be something outside; I feel certain about it."

Weeks cruised by; the peas got yellow, and the shell got yellow.

"All the world is turning yellow, I assume," said they—and maybe they were correct.

Abruptly they felt a draw at the shell. It was removed and held in human hands; at that point, it was slipped into the pocket of a coat, together with other full cases.

"Presently, we will before long be let out," said one, and that was exactly what they all needed.

"I should get a kick out of the chance to know which of us will travel most remote," said the littlest of the five, "and we will before long observe."

"What is to happen will occur," said the biggest pea.

"Split!" went the shell, and the five peas turned out into the splendid daylight. There they lay in a youngster's hand. A young man was holding them firmly.

"Presently, I am flying out into the wide world," said the pea. "Catch me on the off chance that you can." And he was gone in a minute.

"I expect to fly directly to the sun.
"We will rest any place we get ourselves," said the following two; "we will at present be moving onwards." And they fell to the floor and move about, yet they got into the pea-shooter for all that.
"We will go most remote of any," said they.
"What is to happen will occur," shouted the last one, as he was shot out of the pea-shooter. Up he flew against an old load up under a garret window and fell into a little fissure, which was nearly loaded up with greenery and delicate earth. The greenery shut itself about him, and there he lay— a hostage in fact, yet not unnoticed by God.

"What is to happen will occur," said he to himself.

Inside the little garret carried on a poor lady, who went out to clean stoves, hack wood into little pieces, and accomplish other difficult work, for she was both solid and productive. However, she remained constantly poor, and at home in the garret lay her solitary girl, not exactly grown-up and exceptionally sensitive and frail. For an entire year, she had kept her bed, and it appeared as though she could neither bite the dust nor recover.

"She is heading off to her younger sibling," said the lady. "I had just the two children, and it was anything but a simple thing to help them; however, the great God-given to one of them by taking her home to himself. The other was left to me. However, I guess they are not to be isolated, and my wiped out young lady will before long go to her sister in paradise."

Throughout the day, the wiped out young lady lay discreetly and quietly, while her mom went out to procure cash.

Spring came, and mid one morning, the sun shone through the little window and tossed his beams gently and charmingly over the floor of the room. Similarly, as the mother was heading off to her work, they wiped out the young lady fixed her look on the most minimal sheet of the window. "Mother," she shouted, "what can that little green thing be that peeps in at the window? It is moving in the breeze."

The mother ventured to the window and half-opened it. "Goodness!" she stated, "there is, in reality, a little pea that has flourished and is putting out its green leaves. How might it have into this break? Indeed, presently, here is a little nursery for you to interest yourself with." So the bed of the debilitated young lady was moved closer to the window, that she may see the growing plant, and the mother went forward to her work.

"Mother, I trust I will recover," said the debilitated kid at night. "The sun has shone in here so brilliant and warm to-day, and the little pea is developing so fast, that I feel good, as well, and might suspect I will find a workable pace out into the warm daylight once more."

"God award it!" said the mother, yet she didn't know it would be so. She took a stick and then propped up the green plant, which had given her girl such joy, with the goal that it probably won't be broken by the breezes. She tied the bit of string to the window-ledge and to the upper piece of the casing, with the goal that the pea rings may have something to twine around. Furthermore, the plant shot up so fast that one could nearly observe it develop from the everyday.

"A bloom is truly coming," said the mother one morning. Finally, she was starting to let herself trust that her little wiped out girl may undoubtedly recoup. She recalled that for quite a while, the youngster had spoken all the more brightly and that during the most recent couple of days she had brought herself up in bed toward the beginning of the day to look with shining eyes at her little nursery which contained, however, a solitary pea plant.

After seven days, the invalid sat up by the open window an entire hour, feeling very cheerful in the warm daylight, while outside developed the little plant, and on it, a pink pea bloom in full blossom. The little lady twisted down and tenderly kissed the fragile leaves. This day resembled a celebration to her.

"Our magnificent Father himself has planted that pea and caused it to develop and thrive, to carry happiness to you and want to me, my favored kid," said the glad mother, and she grinned at the bloom as though it had been a heavenly attendant from God.

Be that as it may, what was the fate of different peas? Why, the person who flew out into the wide world and stated, "Catch me on the off chance that you can," fell into a drain on the top of a house and finished his movements in the harvest of a pigeon. The two lethargic ones were conveyed very as far and were of some utilization, for they likewise were eaten by pigeons; however the fourth, who needed to arrive at the sun empire, and fell into a sink and lay there in the filthy water for a considerable length of time and weeks, till he had expanded to an incredible size.

"I am getting wonderfully fat," said the pea; "I expect I will blast finally; no pea could accomplish more than that, I might suspect. I am the most exceptional of all the five that were in the shell." And the sink concurred with the pea.

In any case, the little youngster, with shimmering eyes and the ruddy shade of wellbeing upon her cheeks, remained at the open garret window and, collapsing her dainty hands over the pea bloom, expressed gratitude toward God for what He had done.

THE DAISY

In the present time, Out in the nation, near to the side of the road, stood a lovely house; you have seen one like it, presumably, regularly. In front lay a little fenced-in garden, brimming with blossoming blossoms. Close to the fence, in the delicate green grass, grew a little daisy. The sun shone as brilliantly and heartily upon her as upon the huge and wonderful nursery blossoms, so the daisy developed from hour to hour. Each morning she unfurled her little white petals, such as sparkling beams round the brilliant little sun in the focal point of the bloom. She never assumed that she was inconspicuous down in the grass or that she was just a poor, unimportant bloom. She felt too glad to even consider caring for that. Joyfully she moved in the direction of the warm sun, admired the blue sky, and tuned in to the warbler singing high noticeable all around.

One day the little blossom was as cheerful as though it had been an extraordinary occasion, if it was just Monday. All the children were at school, and keeping in mind that they sat on their seats learning their exercises, she, on her little stem, gained likewise from the warm sun and from everything around her how great God is, and it fulfilled her to hear the songbird communicating in his tune her own happy sentiments. The daisy appreciated the upbeat fledgling who could chatter so sweetly and fly so high, and she was not under any condition miserable in light of the fact that she was unable to do likewise.

Inside the nursery grew various blue-blooded blossoms; the less aroma they had, the more they paraded. The peonies thought of it as an amazing thing to be so huge and puffed themselves out to be bigger than the roses. The tulips realized that they were set apart with delightful hues, and held themselves straight as an arrow so they may be seen all the more doubtlessly.

They didn't see the little daisy outside, yet she took a gander at them and thought: "How rich and lovely they are! No big surprise, the pretty fledgling flies down to visit them. How happy I am that I develop so close to them, that I may respect their magnificence!"

Exactly as of now, the warbler flew down, crying "Tweet," yet he didn't go to the tall peonies and tulips; he jumped into the grass close to the modest daisy. She trembled for happiness and barely comprehended what to think. The little winged creature jumped round the daisy, singing, "Gracious, what sweet, delicate grass, and what an exquisite little bloom, with gold in its heart and silver on its dress!" For the yellow community in the Daisy looked like gold, and the leaves around were sparkling white, similar to silver.

How glad the little daisy felt, nobody can depict. The feathered creature kissed her with his nose, sang to her, and afterward flew up again into the blue air above. It was, at any rate, a fourth of an hour prior to the daisy could recuperate herself. Half embarrassed, yet cheerful in herself. She looked at different blossoms; they more likely than not seen the respect she had gotten and would comprehend her joy and delight.

Be that as it may, the tulips looked prouder than any time in recent memory; to be sure, they were clearly very vexed about it. The peonies were nauseated, and might they be able to have spoken, the poor little daisy would no uncertainty have gotten a decent admonishing. She could see they were a full scale of temper, and it made her exceptionally grieved.

As of now, there came into the nursery a young lady with an enormous, sparkling blade in her grasp. She went directly to the tulips and removed a few of them.

"O dear," moaned the daisy, "how stunning! It is done with them now." The young lady diverted the tulips, and the daisy felt exceptionally happy to develop outside in the grass and to be just a poor little bloom. At the point when the sunset, she collapsed up her leaves and rested. She envisioned the entire night long of the warm sun and the truly little winged creature.

The following morning, when she blissfully loosened up her white leaves again to the warm air and the light, she perceived the voice of the winged animal. However, his tune sounded forlorn and dismal.

Oh! He had valid justification for being dismal: he had been gotten and made a detainee in a pen that[16]hung near to the open window. He sang of the glad time when he could fly noticeable all around, happy and free; of the youthful green corn in the fields, from which he would spring ever more elevated to sing his radiant melody—however, now he was a detainee in a confine.

The little daisy wished especially to support him. In any case, what would she be able to do? In her anxiety, she overlooked all the lovely things around her, the warm daylight, and her own entirely, sparkling, white leaves. Oh, dear! She could consider only the hostage winged creature and her own failure to support him.

Two young men left the nursery; one of them conveyed a sharp blade in his grasp, similar to the one with which the young lady had cut the tulips. They went directly to the little daisy, who couldn't think what they would do.

"We can remove a pleasant bit of turf for the warbler here," said one of the young men, and he started to cut a square piece round the daisy, with the goal that she stood just in the middle.
"Pull up the bloom," said the other kid, and the daisy trembled with dread, for to cull her up would pulverize her life, and she wished such a great amount to live and to be taken to the hostage songbird in his pen.

Poor people flying creature was grumbling uproariously about his lost opportunity, beating his wings against the iron bars of his jail. The entire morning went right now.

"There is no water here," said the hostage songbird; "they have all gone out and have neglected to give me a drop to drink. I feel as though I had fire and ice inside me, and the air is so overwhelming. Too bad! I should bite the dust. I should say goodbye to the warm daylight, the crisp green, and all the wonderful things which God has made." And then he pushes his bill into the cool turf to invigorate himself a little with the new grass, and, as he did as such, his eye fell upon the daisy. The flying creature gestured to her and kissed her with his snout and stated: "You additionally will wilt here you poor little bloom! They have offered you to me, with the little fix of green grass on which you develop, in return for the entire world which was mine out there. Every little piece of turf is to me as an incredible tree, and every one of your white leaves a bloom. Oh! you just give me the amount I have lost."

"Goodness, on the off chance that I could just solace him!" thought the daisy, yet she was unable to move a leaf. The scent from her leaves was more grounded than is common in these blossoms, and the flying creature saw it, and however, he was blacking out with thirst, and in his agony pulled up the green pieces of turf, he didn't contact the bloom.

The night came, but nobody had come to bring the fowl a drop of water. At that point, he loosened up his pretty wings and shook convulsively; he could just sing "Tweet, tweet," in a frail, forlorn tone. His little head twisted down toward the bloom; the fowl's heart was broken with need and pining. At that point, the bloom couldn't overlay her leaves as she had done the night prior to when she rested, however, debilitated and dismal, hung toward the earth.

Not till morning did the young men come, and when they found the feathered creature dead, they sobbed numerous and severe tears. They burrowed a really grave for him and decorated it with leaves of blossoms. The winged animal's dead body was set in a shrewd red box and was covered with significant privilege.

Poor feathered creature! While he was still alive and could still sing, they overlooked him and permitted him to sit in his confinement and endure need, yet since he was dead, they grieved for him with numerous tears and covered him in the imperial state.

Be that as it may, the turf with the daisy on it was tossed out into the dusty street. Nobody thought of the little bloom that had felt more for the poor flying creature than had anyone else, and that would have been so happy to help and solace him in the event that she had been capable.

THE FLAX

ONCE UPON A TIME.....

THE flax was in full sprout; it had truly minimal blue blossoms, and the moth is as fragile as the wings. The rain fell on it, and the sun shorne on it, and this was as useful for the flax for what it's worth for little children to be washed and afterward kissed by their moms. They look a lot prettier for it, thus did the flax.

"Individuals state that I look exceedingly well," said the flax, "and that I am so fine and long that I will make an excellent bit of cloth. How lucky I am! It causes me so glad to realize that something can be made of me. How the daylight cheers me, and how sweet and invigorating is the downpour! My joy overwhelms me; nobody on the planet can feel more joyful than I."

"Ok, indeed, most likely," said the greenery, "however you don't have a clue about the world yet just as I do, for my sticks are knotty"; and afterward it sang forlornly:

"Clip, snap, sure,

Basse lure.

The tune is finished."

"No, it isn't finished," said the flax. "To-morrow, the sun will sparkle, or the downpour plummet. I feel that I am developing. I feel that I am in full bloom. I am the most joyful everything being equal, for I may some time or another come to something."

All things considered, one day, a few people came, who grabbed the flax and pulled it by its roots, which was extremely excruciating. At that point, it was laid in water, as though it were to be suffocated, and after that put close to a fire, as though it were to be cooked. This was extremely stunning.

"We can't hope to be glad consistently," said the flax. "By encountering malevolent just as great, we become savvy." And absolutely there was a lot of insidiousness coming up for the flax. It was soaked, and cooked, and broken, and combed; in reality, it hardly realized what was done to it. Finally, it was put on the turning wheel. "Buzz, hum," went the wheel, so rapidly that the flax couldn't gather its musings.

"Indeed, I have been extremely glad," it thought amidst its torment, "and should be mollified with the past." And placated it stayed, till it was put on the loom and turned into a wonderful bit of white material. All the flax, was used to making this one piece.

"All things considered, this is very great," said the flax. "I was unable to have accepted that I ought to be so preferred by fortune. The plant was not off-base when it sang,

'Clip, snap, snurre,

Basse lurre.'

In any case, the melody isn't finished at this point, I am certain; it is just barely starting. How great it is that, after all, I have endured, I am made a big deal about finally! I am the most fortunate individual on the planet—so solid and fine. What's more, how white and long I am! This is obviously better than being an insignificant plant and bearing blossoms. At that point, I had no consideration, nor any water except if it down-poured; presently, I am watched and thought about. Each morning the housekeeper turns me over, and I have a shower from the watering-mug each night. Truly, and the minister's better half saw me and said I was the best bit of material in the entire ward. I can't be more joyful than I am present."

After some time, the material was taken into the house, and they're cut with the scissors and attacked pieces and afterward pricked with needles. This absolutely was not wonderful. However, finally, it was made into twelve articles of clothing of the sort that everyone wears. "See now, at that point," said the flax, "I have become something of significance. This was my predetermination; it is a serious gift. Presently I will be of some utilization on the planet, as each one should be; it is the best way to be glad. I am currently separated into twelve pieces, but the entire dozen is 6 of one, half a dozen of another. It is most uncommon favorable luck."

A long time died, and finally, the material was so worn it could hardly hold together. "We would happily have held together somewhat more, yet it is pointless to anticipate difficulties." And finally, they fell into clothes and wears out and thought it was done with them, for they were torn to shreds and saturated with water and made into a mash and dried, and they knew not what also, till at the same time they got themselves lovely white paper. "Indeed, presently, this is amazement—a wonderful astonishment as well," said the paper. "Presently, I am better than at any other time, and who can determine what fine things I may have composed upon me? This is a brilliant karma!" And so it was, for the most excellent stories and verse were composed upon it, and just used to be there a smudge, which was exceptionally favorable luck. At that point, individuals heard the narratives and verse read, and it made them more astute and better; for every one of that was composed had decent and reasonable importance, and an extraordinary gift was contained in it.

"I envisioned nothing like this when I was just a little blue blossom developing in the fields," said the paper. "How might I realize that I ought to ever be the methods for carrying information and euphoria to men? I can't comprehend it myself, but then it is actually so. Paradise realizes that I have done nothing myself except for what I was obliged to do with my frail forces for my own safeguarding, but then I have been advanced starting with one delight and respect then onto the next. Each time I feel that the melody is finished and afterward, something higher and better starts for me. I guess now I will be conveyed to travel about the world, so individuals may understand me. It can't be something else, for I have more marvelous contemplations composed upon me than I had lovely blossoms in times past. I am more joyful than at any time in recent memory."

However, the paper didn't go on its movements. It was sent later to the printer, and all the words composed inside it were set up in type to make a book,— or rather a large number of books,— for some, more people could get joy and benefit from a printed book than from the composed paper.

"Truly, this is surely the smartest arrangement," said the composed paper; "I truly didn't think about this. I will stay at home and be held in respect like some old granddad, as I truly am to all these new books. They will benefit a few. I was unable to have meandered about as they can, yet he who composed this has taken a gander at me as each word spilled out of his pen upon my surface. I am the most respected of all."
At that point, the paper has connected a group to different papers and tossed into a tub that remained in the washroom.

"After work, it is essential to rest," the paper said, "and an excellent chance to gather one's considerations. Presently I am capable, just because, to realize what is in me; and to realize one's self is genuine advancement. What will be finished with me now, I wonder? Presumably, I will at present go ahead. I have consistently advanced until now, I know very well."

Presently it happened one day that all the paper in the tub was taken out and laid on the hearth to be singed. Individuals said it couldn't be sold at the shop, to wrap up spread and sugar, since it had been composed upon. The children in the house remained round the hearth to watch the blast, for paper consistently blazed up so pleasantly, and a short time later, among the cinders, there were such a significant number of red flashes to be seen pursuing one the other, to a great extent, as speedy as the breeze. They called it seeing the children leave school, and the last sparkle, they stated, was the schoolmaster. They would frequently think the last sparkle had come, and one would cry, "There goes the schoolmaster," however, the following minute, another flash would show up, splendid and excellent how they needed to know where all the sparkles went to! Maybe they will discover some time in the not so distant future.

The entire heap of paper had been set on fire and was before long consuming. "ugh!" It was positively not exceptionally wonderful to be singed. In any case, when the entire was enclosed by flares, the sparkles mounted out of sight, higher than the flax had ever had the option to raise its little blue blossoms, and they shimmered as the white cloth could never have flickered. All the composed letters turned out to be very red in a minute, and all the words and contemplations went to fire.

"Presently, I am mounting straight up to the sun," said a voice in the blazes, and maybe a thousand voices resounded the words as the flares dashed up through the smokestack and went out at the top. At that point, various modest creatures, the same number of as the blossoms on the flax had been, and undetectable to mortal eyes, skimmed over the children. They were significantly lighter and more fragile than the blue blossoms from which they were conceived, and as the flares vanished and nothing was left from the paper, however dark cinders, these little creatures moved upon it, and any place they contacted it, brilliant red sparkles showed up.

"The children are hard and fast of school, and the schoolmaster was the remainder of all," said the children. It was an acceptable enjoyment, and they sang over the dead cinders:

"Clip, snap, snurre,

Basse lurre.

The tune is finished."

Yet, the little imperceptible creatures stated, "The tune is rarely finished; the most lovely is yet to come."

Yet, the children could neither hear nor get this, nor should they, for children, must not know it all.

GOOD NIGHT.........

A CHILD'S DREAM OF STAR

There was before a kid, and he walked around a decent arrangement and thought of various things. He had a sister, who was a youngster as well, and his steady friend. These two used to ponder throughout the day. They stood amazed at the magnificence of the blossoms; they marveled at the stature and blueness of the sky; they marveled at the profundity of the brilliant water; they marveled at the decency and the intensity of God who made the stunning scenery.

They used to state to each other, sometimes, assuming all the children upon earth were to bite the dust, would the blossoms, and the water, and the sky be heartbroken? They accepted they would be heartbroken. The little lively streams that frolic down the sloped sides are the children of the water; and the littlest splendid spots playing at finding the stowaway in the sky throughout the night, should unquestionably be the children of the stars; and they would all be lamented to see their mates, the children of men, no more.

There was one clear sparkling star that used to turn out in the sky before the rest, close to the congregation tower, over the graves. It was bigger and progressively wonderful, they thought than all the others, and consistently they looked for it, standing inseparably at a window. Whoever saw it originally shouted out, "I see the star!" And regularly they shouted out both together, knowing so well when it would rise, and where. So they developed to be such companions with it, that, before resting in their beds, they generally watched out indeed, to offer it a great night; and when they were going round to rest, they used to state, "God favors the star!"

However, while she was still youthful, gracious extremely, youthful, the sister hung, and came to be frail to the point that she could never again remain in the window around evening time; and afterward, the kid watched unfortunately out without anyone else and afterward a grin would happen upon the face, and a feeble little voice used to state, "God favors my sibling and the star!"

Thus the time came very soon! At the point when the youngster peered out alone, and when there was no face on the bed, and when there was somewhat grave among the graves, not there previously, and when the star made long beams down toward him, as he saw it through his tears.

Presently, these beams were so brilliant, and they appeared to make such a sparkling route from earth to Heaven, that when the kid went to his singular bed, he imagined about the star; and envisioned that, lying where he was, he saw a train of individuals taken up that shimmering street by holy messengers. Also, the star, opening, demonstrated him an extraordinary universe of light, where a lot progressively such heavenly attendants held back to get them.

Every one of these blessed messengers, who were pausing, turned their radiating eyes upon the individuals who were conveyed up into the star; and some turned out from the long lines where they stood, and fell upon the individuals' necks, and kissed them delicately, and left with them down roads of light, and we're so glad in their organization, that lying in his bed he sobbed for satisfaction.

His sister's heavenly attendant waited close to the passage of the star, and said to the pioneer among the individuals who had brought the individuals thither:

"Is my sibling come?"

Furthermore, he said, "No."

She was dismissing ideally, when the youngster loosened up his arms, and cried, "O, sister, I am here! Take me!" and afterward, she turned her radiating eyes upon him, and it was night, and the star was sparkling into the room, making long beams down towards him as he saw it through his tears.

From that hour forward, the kid watched. He imagined that he didn't have a place with the earth alone, however to the star as well, in view of his sister's blessed messenger gone previously.

There was an infant destined to be a sibling to the youngster, and keeping in mind that he was little to such an extent that he never yet had verbally expressed word, he extended his minor structure out on his bed and kicked the bucket.

Again the youngster longed for the open star and of the organization of heavenly attendants, and the train of individuals and the columns of holy messengers with their radiating eyes all turned upon those individuals' appearances.

Said his sister's holy messenger to the pioneer:

"Is my sibling come?"

What's more, he said, "Not excessively one, however another."

As the youngster observed his sibling's blessed messenger in her arms, he cried, "O, sister, I am here! Take me!" And she turned and blessed him, and the star was sparkling.

He developed to be a youngster and was occupied at his books when an old hireling came to him and stated:

"Thy mother is no more. I welcome her approval on her sweetheart child!"

Again around evening time, he saw the star and such a previous organization. Said his sister's blessed messenger to the pioneer:

"Is my sibling come?"

Also, he stated, "Thy mother!"

A compelling cry of euphoria went forward through all the star, in light of the fact that the mother was brought together to her two children. Also, he loosened up his arms and cried, "O, mother, sister, and sibling, I am here! Take me!" And they addressed him, "Not yet," and the star was sparkling.

He developed to take care of business, whose hair was turning dark, and he was sitting in his seat by the fireside, substantial with sadness, and with his face bedewed with tears when the star opened by and by.

Said his sister's heavenly attendant to the pioneer: "Does my sibling come?"

What's more, he stated, "Nay, however, his lady little girl."

What's more, the man who had been the youngster saw his little girl, recently lost to him, a heavenly animal among those three, and he stated, "My little girl's head is on my sister's chest, and her arm is around my mom's neck, and at her feet, there is the child of bygone era, and I can manage the splitting from her, God be adulated!"

What's more, the star was sparkling.

In this manner, the kid came to be an elderly person, and his once smooth face was wrinkled, and his means were moderate and weak, and his back was twisted. Also, one night as he lay upon his bed, his children remaining round, he cried....

"I see the star!"

They murmured to each other, "He is kicking the bucket."

What's more, he stated, "I am. My age is tumbling from me like an article of clothing, and I move towards the star as a youngster. Also, O, my Father, presently, I express gratitude toward Thee that it has so frequently opened, to get those darlings who anticipate me!"

What's more, the star was sparkling, and it sparkles upon his grave.

WHAT HAPPENED TO THE THISTLE

AROUND a noble old manor was a lovely, all around kept nursery, brimming with a wide range of uncommon trees and blossoms. Visitors constantly communicated their enjoyment and profound respect at seeing its miracles. The individuals from far and approach used to come on Sundays and occasions and request that authorization see it. Indeed, even entire schools made journeys for the sole reason for seeing its marvels.

Close to the fence that isolated the nursery from the knoll stood a tremendous thorn. It was an exceptionally enormous and fine thorn, with a few branches spreading out simply over the root, and inside and out was so solid and full as to make it well deserving of the name "thorn hedge."

Nobody at any point saw it, spare the old jackass that pulled the milk truck for the dairymaids. He stood eating in the glade hard by and extended his old neck to arrive at the thorn, saying: "You are wonderful! I should get a kick out of the chance to eat you!" But the tie was too short to even think about allowing him to arrive at the thorn, so he didn't eat it.

There were visitors at the Hall, fine, privileged family members from town, and among them a youngster who had originated from a long separation—right from Scotland. She was of an old and respectable family and wealthy in gold and grounds—a lady of the hour certainly justified regardless of the triumphant, thought more than one youngster to himself; indeed, and their moms thought in this way, as well!

The youngsters delighted themselves on the grass, playing croquet and fluttering about among the blossoms, every little youngster assembling a bloom to place in the buttonhole of somebody of the respectable men.

The youthful Scotch woman searched about for a blossom. However, none of them appeared to satisfy her until, happening to look over the fence, she espied the fine, huge thorn bramble, brimming with pale blue red, durable looking blossoms. She grinned from her perspective and asked the child of the house to get one of them for her.

"That is Scotland's bloom," she said; "it develops and blooms in our ensign. Get that one there for me. It would be ideal if you.

What's more, he accumulated the best of the thorn blossoms. However, he pricked his fingers as much in doing as such as though it had been developing on a wild rosebush.

She took the blossom and put it in his buttonhole, which caused him to feel extraordinarily regarded. Every one of the other youngsters would happily have surrendered his smooth nursery bloom on the off chance that he may have worn the one given by the fragile hands of the Young Scotch lady. As distinctly as the child of the house felt the respect presented upon him, the thorn felt significantly more exceptionally regarded. It appeared to feel dew and daylight experiencing it.

"It appears I am of more result than I suspected," it said to itself. "I should start by the right to remain inside and not outside the fence. One gets unusually set right now, presently I have in any event one of my blossoms over the fence—and there, yet in a buttonhole!"

To every last one of its buds, as it opened, the thorn shrub told this incredible occasion. What's more, very few days had gone before it heard—not from the individuals who passed, nor yet from the twittering of little fowls, however from the air, which gives out, far and wide, the sounds that it has cherished up from the shadiest strolls of the delightful nursery and from the most detached rooms at the Hall, where entryways and windows are left open—that the youngster who got the thorn blossom from the hands of the Scottish lady had gotten her heart and hand also.

"That is my doing!" said the thorn, thinking about the bloom she had given to the buttonhole. What's more, every new blossom that came was recounted this great occasion.

"Doubtlessly, I will presently be taken and planted in the nursery," thought the thorn. "Maybe I will be placed into a flowered mug, for that is by a wide margin the fairest position." It thought of this so long it finished by saying to itself with the firm conviction of truth, "I will be planted in a flowered mug!"

It guaranteed each and every bud that came that it additionally ought to be put in a mug and maybe have a spot in a buttonhole—that being the most noteworthy position one could strive for. None of them got into a flowered mug, and still less into a man of his word's buttonhole.

They lived on light and air and savored daylight the day and dew around evening time. They got visits from honey bee and hornet, who came to search for the nectar in the bloom, and who took the nectar and left the blossom.

"The bum colleagues," said the thorn hedge. "I would puncture them on the off chance that I could!"

The blossoms hung and blurred. However, new ones consistently came.

"You come as though you had been sent," said the thorn hedge to them. "I am anticipating that each minute should be assumed control over the fence."

Several innocuous daisies and a gigantic, slight plant of canary grass tuned in to this with the most profound regard, accepting all they heard. The old jackass that needed to pull the milk truck, cast yearning, looked toward the sprouting thorn and attempted to arrive at it, yet his tie was excessively short. What's more, the thorn shrub thought and thought, so much thus long, of the Scotch thorn—to whom it trusted itself related—that finally, it liked it had originated from Scotland and that its folks had developed into the Scottish arms.

It was an incredible idea. However, an extraordinary thorn may well have extraordinary contemplations.

"Sometimes one is of respectable race regardless of whether one doesn't have any acquaintance with it," said the annoy developing near to—it had a sort of presentiment that it may be transformed into muslin if appropriately treated.

The late spring passed, and the harvest time passed; the leaves tumbled from the trees; the blossoms accompanied more grounded hues and less aroma; the plant specialist's fellow sang on the opposite side of the fence:

"Up the slope and down the slope,

That is the method for the world still."

The youthful pine trees in the wood started to feel a yearning for Christmas. However, Christmas was as yet far off.

"Here I am still," said the thorn. "It appears that I am very overlooked, but it was I who made the match. They were locked in, and now they are hitched—the wedding was seven days back. I don't make a solitary advance forward, for I can't."

Half a month passed. The thorn had its last, single blossom, which was enormous and full and becoming down close to the root. The breeze blew briskly over it, the shading blurred, and all its brilliance vanished, leaving just the cup of the blossom, presently become as extensive as the bloom of artichoke and shimmering like a silvered sunflower.

The youthful couple, who were presently man and spouse, tagged along the nursery way, and as they went close to the fence, the lady, looking over it, stated, "Why, there stands the enormous thorn! it has no blossoms now."

"Indeed, there is as yet the phantom of the last one," said her better half, highlighting the gleaming survives from the last bloom—a blossom in itself.

"How lovely it is!" she said. "We should have one cut in the casing of our image."

Also, again the youngster needed to get over the fence, to sever the shiny cup of the thorn blossom. It pricked his fingers for his agonies since he had considered it an apparition. And afterward, it was brought into the nursery, and to the Hall, and into the drawing-room. There stood an enormous picture—the representations of the two, and in the groom's buttonhole was painted a thorn. They discussed it, and of the bloom cup they had gotten with them—the last silver-gleaming thorn blossom, that should have been repeated in the cutting of the casing.

The air took every one of their words and dispersed them about, far and wide.

"What bizarre things transpire!" said the thorn shrub. "My first-conceived went to live in a buttonhole, my last-conceived in a casing! I wonder what is to happen to me."

The old jackass, remaining by the side of the road, cast cherishing looked at the thorn and stated, "Come to me, my darling, for I can't go to you; my tie is excessively short!"

Be that as it may, the thorn hedge made no answer. It developed increasingly keen, and it thought as a long way ahead as Christmas, till its growing contemplations opened into bloom.

"At the point when one's children are securely housed, a mother is very substantial to remain past the fence."

"That is valid," said the daylight, "and you will be all around set, never dread."

"In a flowered mug or in a casing?" asked the thorn.

GOOD NIGHT.................

THE BUCKWHEAT

On the off chance that YOU should risk, after a whirlwind, to cross a field where buckwheat is developing, you may see that it looks dark and seared, as though a fire of fire had disregarded it. Furthermore, should you ask the explanation, a rancher will let you know, "The lightning did that."

In any case, how is it that the lightning did it?

I will mention to you what the sparrow let me know, and the sparrow heard it from a matured willow which stood—and still represents that issue—near the field of buckwheat.
This willow is tall and admired, however old and injured. Its trunk is part clear through the center, and grass and blackberry rings creep out through the separated. The tree twists forward, and its branches hang like long, green hair.

In the fields around the willow developed rye, wheat, and oats—lovely oats that, when ready, seemed as though minimal yellow canary flying creatures sitting on a branch. The collect had been honored, and the more full the ears of grain, the lower they bowed their heads in respectful quietude.

There was likewise a field of buckwheat lying just before the old willow. The buckwheat didn't bow its head, similar to the remainder of the grain, yet stood erect in tenacious pride.

"I am very as rich as the oats," it said, "and, additionally, I am substantially more sightly. My blossoms are as lovely as apple blooms. It is a treat to take a gander at me and my allies. Old willow, do you know much else excellent than we?"

The willow gestured his head, as much as to state, "Undoubtedly I do!" But the buckwheat was so puffed proudly that it just stated: "The idiotic tree! He is old to the point that grass is becoming out of his body."

Presently there went ahead an awful tempest, and the blossoms of the field collapsed their leaves or bowed their heads as it disregarded them. The buckwheat blossom alone stood erect in the entirety of its pride.

"Bow your heads," called the blossoms as we all do.

"There is no requirement for me to do that," addressed the buckwheat.

"The blessed messenger of tempests comes flying here. He has wings that reach from the mists to the earth; he will destroy you before you have the opportunity to ask for leniency."

"In any case, I don't decide to bow down," said the buckwheat.

"Close your blossoms and crease your leaves," said the old willow. "Try not to take a gander at the lightning when the cloud breaks. Indeed, even people dare not do that, for, amidst the lightning, one may look straight into God's paradise. The sight strikes people daze, so amazing, is it? What might not transpire, negligible plants of the field, who are such a lot humbler, on the off chance that we should set out do as such?"

"So a lot, humbler! For sure! On the off chance that there is an opportunity, I will look directly into God's paradise." And in its pride and haughtiness, it did as such. The flashes of lightning were terrible to the point that it appeared as though the entire world were on fire.

At the point when the storm was finished, both the grain and the blossoms, enormously invigorated by the downpour, again stood erect in the unadulterated, calm air. Be that as it may, the buckwheat had been scorched as dark as ash by the lightning and remained in the field like a dead, futile weed.

The old willow waved his branches back and forth in the breeze, and enormous drops of water tumbled from his green leaves, as though he were crying tears. The sparrows asked: "For what reason would you say you are sobbing when all-around appears to be fortunate? Do you not smell the sweet fragrance of blossoms and shrubs? The sun sparkles, and the mists have gone from the sky. For what reason do you sob, old tree?"

At that point, the willow let them know of the buckwheat's difficult pride and of the discipline which followed.

I, who tell this story, heard it from the sparrows. They told it one night when I had approached them for a story.

The Pen and The Inkstand

Quite a while back, in an artist's room, where his inkstand remained on the table, the comment was once made: "It is awesome what can be brought out of an inkstand. What will come to straightaway? It is, without a doubt, magnificent."

"Indeed, positively," said the inkstand to the pen and to different articles that remained on the table; "that is the thing that I generally state. It is brilliant and exceptional what various things leave me. It's very unbelievable, and I actually never recognize what is coming next when that man plunges his pen into me. One drop out of me is sufficient for a large portion of a page of paper—and what can't a large portion of a page contain?

"From me, all crafted by the writer are created—each one of those nonexistent characters whom individuals extravagant they have known or met, and all the profound inclination, the silliness, and the striking pictures of nature. I myself don't see how it is, for I am not familiar with nature, yet it is surely in me. From me have gone forward to the world those superb depictions of enchanting ladies, and of valiant knights on skipping steeds; of the stop and the visually impaired—and I know not what more, for I guarantee you I never think about these things."

"There you are correct," said the pen, "for you don't think by any stretch of the imagination. On the off chance that you did, you would see that you can just give the methods. You give the liquid that I may put upon the paper that abides in me and what I wish to expose. The pen composes. No man questions that, and to be sure the vast majority comprehend as much about verse as an old inkstand."

"You have had next to no understanding," answered the inkstand. "You have barely been in administration a week and are as of now half exhausted. Do you envision you are an artist? You are just a hireling, and before you came, I had many like you. I realize a plume pen just as I probably am aware of a steel one. I have had the two sorts in my administration, and I will have a lot more as long as he comes—the man who plays out the mechanical part—and records what he acquires from me. I should get a kick out of the chance to recognize what will be the following thing he escapes me."

"Inkmug!" answered the pen disdainfully.

Late at night, the artist got back from a show, where he had been very captivated by the commendable execution of a well-known violin player.

The player had created from his instrument a wealth of tone that sometimes seemed as though tinkling water drops or moving pearls, sometimes like the flying creatures twittering in melody, and afterward once more, rising and expanding like a breeze through the fir trees. The artist felt as though his own heart were sobbing; however, in tones of tune, similar to the sound of a lady's voice. These sounds appeared to come from the strings as well as from all aspects of the instrument. It was a great presentation and a troublesome piece, but then the bow appeared to skim over the strings so effectively that one would figure anyone could do it. The violin and the bow appeared to be autonomous of their lord, who guided them. Maybe the soul and soul had been inhaled into the instrument. Furthermore, the crowd overlooked the entertainer in the wonderful sounds he delivered.

Not all that the artist; he recalled that he and recorded his contemplations regarding the matter: "How absurd it would be for the violin and the bow to flaunt their presentation, but we men regularly submit that imprudence. The writer, the craftsman, the man of science in his research center, the general—we as a whole do it, but then we are just the instruments which the Almighty employments. To only him, respect is expected. We don't have anything in ourselves of which we ought to be glad." Yes, this is the thing that the artist composed. He composed it as a story and called it "The Master and the Instruments."
"That is the thing that you get, madam," said the pen to the inkstand when the two were distant from everyone else once more. "Did you hear him read so anyone might hear what I had recorded?"

"Truly, what I offered you to compose," countered the inkstand. "That was a cut at you, in view of your arrogance. Imagine that you couldn't comprehend that you were being tested! I gave you a cut from inside me. Without a doubt, I should know my own parody."

"Ink, pitcher!" cried the pen.

"Composing stick!" answered the inkstand. Also, every one of them felt fulfilled that he had offered a decent response. It is satisfying to be persuaded that you have settled an issue with your answer; it is something to make you rest soundly. What's more, the two of them rested soundly over it.

Be that as it may, the artist didn't rest. Considerations rose inside him, similar to the tones of the violin, falling like pearls or surging like the solid breeze through the backwoods. He comprehended his own heart in these contemplations; they were as a beam from the brain of the Great Master all things considered.

"To Him be all the respect."
GOOD NIGHT..........................

THE TEAMUG

THERE was before a pleasing tea mug; it was glad for being porcelain, glad for its long spout, pleased with its expansive handle. It had something previously and behind— the spout previously and the handle behind— and that was what it discussed. In any case, it didn't discuss its top, which was split and bolted; these were deformities, and one doesn't discuss one's imperfections, for there are a lot of others to do that. The cups, the cream mug, and the sugar bowl, the entire lunch service, would think much oftener of the top's defects—and discussion about them—than of the sound handle and the wonderful spout. The tea mug knew it.

"I know you," it said inside itself. "I know, as well, my flaw, and I am very much aware that in that very thing is seen my quietude, my unobtrusiveness. Flaws we as a whole have, yet we likewise have remunerations. The cups have a handle, the sugar bowl a cover; I have both, and one thing additionally, in front, which they can never have. I have a spout, and that makes me the sovereign of the coffee table. I spread abroad a gift on thirsting humankind, for, in me, the Chinese leaves are fermented in the bubbling, boring water."
This said the tea mug in its crisp youthful life. It remained on the table that was spread for tea; it was lifted by an extremely sensitive hand, yet the fragile hand was cumbersome. The tea mug fell, the spout snapped off, and the handle snapped off. The cover was no more terrible at all; the most noticeably awful had been discussed that.

The tea mug lay in a swoon on the floor, while the bubbling water came up short on it. It was a frightful disgrace, yet the most noticeably awful was that everyone scoffed at it; they sneered at the tea mug and not at the cumbersome hand.

"I never will overlook that experience," said the tea mug, when it a short time later discussed its life. "I was called an invalid, and set in a corner, and the following day was given to a lady who asked for victuals. I fell into destitution and stood moronic both outside and in. Yet, at that point, similarly, as I seemed to be, started my better life. One can be a certain something and still become very another.

"Earth was set in me. For a tea mug, this is equivalent to being covered; however, in the earth was set a blossom bulb. Who put it there, who gave it, I know not; yet given it was, and it turned into pay for the Chinese leaves and the bubbling water, pay for the messed up handle and spout.

"Also, the bulb lay in the earth. The bulb lay in me; it turned into my heart, my living heart, for example, I had at no other time had. There was life in me, power, and may. The heartbeat and the bulb set forth grows; it was the jumping up of considerations and emotions which burst forward into bloom.

"I saw it, I bore it, I overlooked myself in its enjoyment. Favored is it to overlook oneself in another. The bloom gave me not this time; it didn't consider me. It was appreciated and lauded, and I was happy at that. How cheerful it probably been! One day I heard somebody state that the bloom merited a superior mug. I was pounded hard on my back, which was an incredible tribulation, and the bloom was placed into a superior mug. I was tossed out into the yard, where I lie as an old mugsherd. Yet, I have the memory, and that I can never lose."

THE FARMYARD COCK AND THE WEATHERCOCK

THERE were once two roosters; one of them remained on a dunghill, the other on the rooftop. Both were vain, yet the inquiry is, Which of the two was the more valuable?

A wooden segment separated the poultry-yard from another yard, in which lay a stack of fertilizer protecting a cucumber bed. Right now, a huge cucumber, which was completely mindful that it was a plant that ought to be raised in a hotbed.

"It is the benefit of birth," said the Cucumber to itself. "All can't be conceived cucumbers; there must be different sorts too. The fowls, the ducks, and the cows in the following yard are, for the most part, various animals, and there is the yard rooster—I can admire him when he is on the wooden parcel. He is sure of a lot more prominent significance than the weathercock, who is so exceptionally set, and who can't squeak significantly less crow—also, he has neither hens nor chickens, and considers just himself, and sweats verdigris. However, the yard cockerel is something like a rooster. His step resembles a move, and his crowing is music, and any place he goes it is in a flash known. What a trumpeter he is! On the off chance that he would just come in here! Regardless of whether he was to gobble me up, stalk and all, it would be a lovely passing." So said the Cucumber.

During the night, the climate turned out to be awful; hens, chickens, and even the cockerel himself looked for cover. The breeze blew down with an accident the segment between the two yards, and the tiles came tumbling from the rooftop. However, the weathercock stood firm. He didn't turn round; actually, he proved unable, in spite of the fact that he was new and recently cast. He had been brought into the world fully developed and didn't at all look like the feathered creatures, for example, the sparrows and swallows that fly underneath the vault of paradise. He loathed them and viewed them as meager twittering winged creatures that were made distinctly to sing. The pigeons, he conceded, were huge and shone in the sun like mother-of-pearl. They, to some degree, took after weathercocks. However, they were fat and moronic and considered just stuffing themselves with nourishment. "Other than," said the weathercock, "they are tedious things to speak with."

The winged animals of section regularly visited the weathercock and revealed to him tales of remote terrains, of huge rushes going through the air, and of experiences with looters and feathered creatures of prey. These were extremely intriguing when heard just because, yet, the weathercock realized the feathered creatures constantly rehashed themselves, and that made it repetitive to tune in.

"They are repetitive, as is each one else," said he; "there is nobody fit to connect with. Every last one of them is wearisome and idiotic. The entire world merits nothing—it is comprised of idiocy."

The weathercock was what is classified "grand," and that quality alone would have made him fascinating according to the Cucumber, had she known it. Be that as it may, she had eyes just for the yard chicken, who had really shown up in her yard, for the viciousness of the tempest had passed, yet the breeze had blown down the wooden palings.

"What's your opinion of that for crowing?" solicited the yard cockerel from his hens and chickens. It was a somewhat harsh and needed style. However, they didn't say as much, as they ventured upon the dunghill while the rooster swaggered about as though he had been a knight. "Nursery plant," he cried to the Cucumber. She heard the words with profound inclination, for they indicated that he comprehended what her identity was, and she overlooked that he was pecking at her and gobbling her up—a cheerful passing!

At that point, the hens came running up, and the chickens followed, for where one runs the rest run moreover. They clacked and trilled and took a gander at the rooster and were pleased that they had a place with him. "Rooster a-doodle-doo!" crowed he; "the chickens in the poultry-yard will develop to be huge fowls in the event that I make my voice heard on the planet."

What's more, the hens and chickens clacked and tweeted, and the rooster disclosed to them an incredible bit of news. "A rooster can lay an egg," he said. "Furthermore, what do you believe is in that egg? In that egg lies a basilisk. Nobody can persevere through seeing a basilisk. Men know my capacity, and now you comprehend what I am prepared to do, likewise, and what a famous flying creature I am." And with this, the yard rooster fluttered his wings, raised his brush, and crowed once more, till all the hens and chickens trembled; yet they were glad that one of their race ought to be of such eminence on the planet. They clacked, and they peeped with the goal that the weathercock heard it; he had heard everything, except had not mixed.

"It's all dumb stuff," said a voice inside the weathercock. "The yard chicken doesn't lay eggs anything else than I do, and I am excessively lethargic. I could lay a breeze egg in the event that I enjoyed, yet the world does not merit a breeze egg. What's more, presently, I don't plan to stay here anymore."

With that, the weathercock severed and fell into the yard. He didn't execute the yard cockerel, despite the fact that the hens said he planned to do as such.

Also, what does the ethical state? "Preferable to crow over to be vainglorious and separate finally."

THE RED SANDAL

THERE was at one time an entirely sensitive young lady, who was poor to such an extent that she needed to go shoeless in summer and wear a coarse wooden shoe in winter, which made her little instep very red.

In the focal point of the town, there experienced an old shoemaker's better half. One day this great lady made, just as she could, a little pair of shoes out of certain pieces of old red material. The shoe was sufficiently awkward, certainly, yet they fitted the young lady passably well, and in any case, the lady's goal was benevolent. The young lady's name was Martial.

On the very day that Martial got the shoe, her mom was to be covered. They were not in any way reasonable for grieving, yet she had no others, so she put them on her little uncovered feet and followed the poor, plain casket to its last resting place.

Exactly at that time, an enormous, good old carriage happened to cruise by, and the old woman who sat in it saw the young lady and felt sorry for her.

"Give me the young lady," she said to the priest, "and I will deal with her."

Martial assumed that this happened due to the red shoe. However, the old woman believed them shocking and requested them to be singed. Martal was then wearing flawless, well-fitting garments and educated to peruse and sew. Individuals revealed to her she was pretty, yet the mirror stated, "You are considerably more than lovely—you are delightful."

It happened not long a while later that the sovereign and her little girl, the princess, went through the land. All the individuals, Martal among the rest, rushed toward the castle and swarmed around it, while the little princess, wearing white, remained at the window for each one to see. She wore neither a train nor a brilliant crown, yet on her feet were lovely red morocco shoes, which, it must be conceded, were prettier than those the shoemaker's significant other had given to little Martal. Definitely, nothing on the planet could be contrasted with that red shoe.

Presently that Martal was mature enough to be affirmed, she obviously needed to have another gown and new shoe. The shoemaker took the proportion of her little feet in his own home, in a room where stood incredible glass cases loaded up with a wide range of fine shoe and exquisite, sparkling boots. It was a pretty sight, yet the old woman couldn't see well and normally didn't enjoy such a great amount of it as Martal. Among the shoe were a couple of red ones, much the same as those ragged by the little princess.

"Are they of cleaned cowhide, that they sparkle so?" asked the old woman.
"Truly, in reality, they do sparkle," answered Martal. What's more, since they fitted her, they were purchased. Yet, the old woman had no clue that they were red, or she could never on the planet have permitted Martal to go to affirmation in them, as she currently did. Each one, obviously, took a gander at Martal's shoe; and when she strolled up the nave to the chancel her couldn't help thinking that even the antique figures on the landmarks, the pictures of pastors and their spouses, with their solid ruffs and long dark robes, were focusing on her red shoe. In any event, when the minister laid his hand upon her head and talked about her contract with God and how she should now start to be a fully-developed Christian, and when the organ chimed forward seriously, and the children's crisp, sweet voices got together with those of the ensemble—still Martal thought of only her shoe.

Toward the evening, when the old woman heard each one talk about the red shoe, she said it was stunning and ill-advised and that, later on, when Martal went to the chapel, it should consistently be in dark shoe, regardless of whether they were old.

The following Sunday was Martal's first Communion day. She saw her dark shoe and afterward at her red ones, on the other hand, at the dark, and at the red—and the red ones were put on.

The sun shone splendidly, and Martal and the old woman strolled to chapel through the cornfields, for the street was dusty.

At the entryway of the congregation stood an old officer who inclined upon a bolster and had magnificently long whiskers that were not white, however red. He bowed nearly to the ground and inquired as to whether he may tidy her shoe. Martal, in her turn, put out her little foot.

"Goodness, look, what keen small moving siphons!" said the old trooper. "Psyche, you don't neglect them off when you move," and he ignored his hands them. The old woman gave the warrior a half-penny and went with Martal into the congregation.

As in the past, each one saw Martal's red shoe, and all the cut figures too bowed their look upon them. When Martal stooped at the chancel, she thought distinctly about the shoe; they glided before her eyes, and she neglected to state her petition or sing her hymn.

Finally, all the individuals left the congregation, and the old woman got into her carriage. As Martal lifted her foot to step in, the old fighter stated, "See what beautiful moving shoe!" And

Martal, despite herself, made a couple of moving advances. At the point when she had once started, her feet went on of themselves; it was just as the shoe had gotten control over her. She moved around the congregation corner— she was unable to support it— and the coachman needed to run behind and get her to place her into the carriage. Still, her feet continued moving, along these lines, that she trod upon the great woman's toes. It was not until the shoe was taken from her feet that she had rest.

The shoe was taken care of in a storeroom. However, Martial couldn't avoid going to take a gander at them occasionally.

Not long after this, the old woman lay sick in bed, and it was said that she was unable to recuperate. She must be breastfed and looked out for, and this, obviously, was nobody's obligation to such an extent as it was Martial's, as Martal herself no doubt understood. In any case, there happened to be an extraordinary ball in the town, and Martal was welcomed. She took a gander at the old woman, who was exceptionally sick, and she took a gander at the red shoe.

Bizarre to state, when she needed to move to the privilege, the shoe bore her to one side; and when she wished to move up the room, the shoe continued going down the room. Down the stairs, they conveyed her finally, into the road, and out through the town door. Endlessly she moved, for the move she should, straight out into the bleak wood. Up among the trees, something shimmered. It was the old fighter with the red whiskers, who sat and gestured, saying, "See what beautiful moving shoe!"

She was frightfully scared and attempted to discard the red shoe, yet they clung fast, and she was unable to unclasp them. They appeared to have developed fast to her feet. So move she should, and move she did, over field and glade, in the downpour and in daylight, around evening time and by day—and around evening time it was by a long shot increasingly shocking.

She moved out away from any confining influence churchyard. However, the dead there didn't move; they were very still and had much better activities.
She moved past the open church entryway, and there she saw a heavenly attendant in long white robes and with wings that came to from his shoulders to the earth. His look was harsh and grave, and in his grasp, he held a wide, sparkling sword.

"Thou shalt move," he stated, "in thy red shoe, till thou workmanship pale and cold, and till thy body is squandered like a skeleton. Thou shalt move from entryway to entryway, and any place glad, haughty children abide thou shalt thump, that, hearing thee, they may take cautioning. Move thou shalt—move on!"

"Benevolence!" cried Martial; however, she didn't hear the appropriate response of the heavenly attendant, for the shoe conveyed her past the entryway and on into the fields.

One morning she moved past a notable entryway. Inside was the sound of a song, and by and by a pine box strewn with blossoms was borne out. She realized that her companion, the old woman, was dead, and in her heart, she felt that she was deserted by all on earth and censured by God's blessed messenger in paradise.

Still on, she moved—for she was unable to stop—through thistles and briers, while her feet drained. At long last, she moved to a desolate little house where she realized that the killer abided, and she tapped at the window, saying, "Turn out, turn out! I can't come in, for I should move."

The man stated, "Do you know who I am and what I do?"

"Indeed," said Martal; "yet don't strike off my head, for then I was unable to live to apologize for my wrongdoing. Strike off my feet, that I might be freed of my red shoe."

At that point, she admitted her transgression, and the killer struck off the red shoe, which moved away over the fields and into the profound wood. To Martal, it appeared that the feet had gone with the shoe, for she had nearly lost the intensity of strolling.

"Presently I have languished enough over the red shoe," she said; "I will go to the congregation, that individuals may see me." But no sooner had she tottered to the congregation entryway than the shoe moved before her and alarmed her back.

All that week, she persevered through the quickest distress and shed many severe tears. At the point when Sunday came, she stated: "I am certain I probably endured and endeavored enough at this point. I am very as acceptable. I dare say, the same number of who are holding their heads high in the congregation." So she took mental fortitude and went once more. In any case, before she arrived at the churchyard entryway, the red shoe was moving there, and she turned around again in dread, more profoundly sad than any time in recent memory for her transgression.

She, at that point, went to the minister's home and asked out of consideration for being taken into the family's administration, promising to be tireless and loyal. She didn't need compensation, she stated, just a home with great individuals. The priest's better half felt sorry for her and conceded her solicitation, and she demonstrated innovative and attentive.

Genuinely she listened when at night the evangelist read so anyone might hear the Holy Scriptures. All the children came to cherish her; however, when they talked about magnificence and luxury, she would shake her head and dismiss.

On Sunday, when they all went to chapel, they inquired as to whether she would not go, as well, yet she looked tragic and bade them abandon her. At that point, she went to her own little room, and as she sat with the hymn book in her grasp, perusing its pages with a delicate, devout psyche, the breeze brought her the notes of the organ. She raised her mournful eyes and stated, "O God, do thou help me!"

At that point, the sun shone brilliantly, and before her stood the white, blessed messenger that she had seen at the congregation entryway. He never again bore the sparkling sword, however in his grasp was an excellent part of roses. He contacted the roof with it, and the roof rose, and at each spot where the branch contacted it, there shone a star. He contacted the dividers, and they augmented so that Martal could see the organ that was being played at the congregation. She saw, as well, the old pictures and statues on the dividers, and the gathering sitting in the seats and singing songs, for the congregation itself had gone to the poor young lady in her restricted room, or she in her chamber had come to it. She sat in the seat with the remainder of the priest's family, and when the hymn was finished, they gestured and stated, "Thou didst well to come, Martal!"

"This is leniency," said she. "It is the finesse of God."

The organ chimed, and the melody of children's voices blended sweetly with it. The splendid daylight shed its warm light, through the windows, over the seat wherein Martal sat. Her heart was so loaded up with daylight, harmony, and delight that it broke, and her spirit was borne by a sunbeam up to God, where there was no one to get some information about the red shoe.

THE SOUP PRINCESS

Quite a while in the past, in a realm far away, experienced the wonderful Princess Mariam who lived with her bereaved dad, the lord in a royal residence on a slope.

Mariam was similarly as a princess ought to be, wonderful, cunning, neighborly, somewhat littler than most young ladies her age and perhaps only somewhat difficult (on the off chance that she believed she wasn't getting what she needed), and there was one thing she needed more than anything on the planet... more than her five white ponies... more than her 20 silk dresses ... considerably more than her 50 sets of hand-made shoes... .

SOUP
The excellent Princess Mariam enjoyed soup... no... she LOVED soup... vegetable soup meat soup, meager soup, thick soup, hot soup, cold soup, zesty soup, flat soup, cream sou.. (Well, you get the thought).

Presently nobody truly knows why Mariam preferred soup so a lot – however, many states it was a direct result of what befell her when she was a young lady.

ice skater

Mariam had sneaked out of the royal residence and was playing on a solidified lake close by, as she played, she slipped, and fell through some meager ice, into freezing water.

She would have suffocated as well, on the off chance that she wasn't spared by two young men, who hauled her to wellbeing.

The three would have become extraordinary companions, yet the young men started contending (absolutely overlooking the shuddering princess), and before the princess could express gratitude toward them, she was hurried back to the royal residence and given a cup of soup.

soup

As she ate the soup, she thought of the two young men that had spared her and appreciated the soup VERY a lot... since the time that day, she would have soup at whatever point she could.

The years passed by, and as it moved toward the Princesses 21st Birthday, the King's musings – as King's considerations regularly do – went to the marriage of his lone girl and finding a reasonable prince for Mariam.

princesuiter

The King was a delicate and adoring man, regularly skirting significant state occasions so as to help Mariam with her riding or hand conveying some soup while she painted her photos... of soup.

At the point when she wasn't eating soup, she was riding the ponies around the domain... she cherished everything in her life, yet she found the suitors her dad exhibited to her, exhausting and uninteresting.

She adored her dad without a doubt yet couldn't wed for the good of him... .she needed somebody unique... .and she could pause!.

Mariam was astute, and she had a thought... as she adored her dad and realized how significant this was to him, she consented to wed on one condition;

The man she would wed would need to have the option to cook the best soup on the planet.

The King considered over this for quite a while... scratching his long facial hair somewhere down in thought... .it was more troublesome than the King had the first idea after all, Mariam was somewhat a specialist regarding the matter.

ruler

The King investigated his glasses and his little girl and grinned...

"Do you know... " he said in his delicate, however profound voice...

"I imagine that is a generally excellent thought !"

The King set about telling the Kingdom... conveying banners over the land – offering his girls turn in marriage if a man could cook the world's ideal soup.

Obviously, there was incredible intrigue, the deals of cookery books shot up, nourishment racks were exposed, as would-be culinary specialists made a decent attempt to consummate the "best soup on the planet."

chef stove

Presently to a culinary expert, this was a test, and particularly to Barry Gorge, who was a standout amongst other Chefs in the land ... who, as it occurred, lived in the neighboring town.

Barry was not an ugly man – but rather he minded not to dazzle individuals through the manner in which he looked, he needed to be acknowledged for the manner in which he cooked..!

chef mug

He had watched the path of gourmet specialists, princes, and would-be Kings walk up the slope with trusts high, just to restore a couple of moments later with dismal faces and void dishes.

Barry invested this energy idealizing his soup, long periods of training, and decent notoriety made him the most loved in the race to make Mariam his significant other.

Honestly, Barry had no enthusiasm for Mariam, his fantasy was to be perceived as the best culinary expert in the land, and this was his opportunity of a lifetime.

Three weeks had passed, and the King was getting disappointed with the postponement, he looked out for Mariam as each confident, bowed nimbly, ignored a bowl of soup, and paused.

They were frequently too eager to even think about watching, as Mariam consistently sneered the parcel! (All things considered, she enjoyed great soup and awful soup).

The King obviously would know straight away the result, Mariam didn't need to talk, she pushed the bowl away and cleaned her mouth, she would spoil her nose like a mouse and state "thank you that was decent... yet I have tasted better."

chef soup

At the point when it went to Barry's chance, there was a buzz that circumvented the castle, swarms accumulated, and wished him well as he started the long stroll up the slope to the royal residence.

Those that didn't have any acquaintance with him would have thought he was the weirdest of characters, a scruffy looking individual ... humiliated ... huffing and puffing as he climbed... as it did, all things considered, take him longer than most... .he before long started to lament the long stretches of inspecting his own cooking.

Mariam created her uncommon spoon and took a tad bit of the soup and smelt it. She grinned, the King grinned, Barry gestured (feeling pompous).

silver spoon

She shut her eyes and took a taste….

"Well, exquisite," she said.

The King applauded… the workers in the royal residence cheered…

However, as the King went to shake Barry's hand, Mariam intruded on them.

"However, " she stated, delayed then unobtrusively "… there's something missing… ."

Barry couldn't accept his ears, he turned out to be extremely red and exceptionally cross, rapidly (as culinary specialists do !)

"Something is missing ?!?," he yelled.

He pushed away from the platter and bowl and stepped out of the royal residence, bursting the entirety of the hirelings out of his way.

The hirelings returned to their work, the King constrained a grin, turned his back, and hit the hay.

Just Mariam stayed at the table attempting to spare the soup which had been tipped on the table, all things considered, it was acceptable soup!

From outside the regal windows, a shadowy figure gazed at the princess and afterward vanished after the Chef into the town.

Barry was seething; he didn't see the workers he pushed off the beaten path, or the groups hanging tight for him in the town, or the "Ruler Barry" banners that had been set up outside his eatery.

He additionally didn't see the shadowy figure tail him down the dull rear entryway behind the enormous kitchen of his eatery.

As he entered the Kitchen through the indirect access, he plunked down crumbling against his mugs and skillet, his head in his grasp.

He more likely than not nodded off as he was unexpectedly alarmed by a clamor in the yard – he hopped up with a beginning and crawled towards the entryway with a wooden spoon and glass blending bowl – prepared to stand up to what he thought was a wanderer hound that was rummaging for titbits tossed by the kitchen staff.

He opened the indirect access and went into the yard.

Nothing.

As he reappeared the kitchen and shut the entryway behind him, he encountered the secretive outsider… .he dropped the bowl…

SMASHHHHHH!!!!!!

Just it was no more abnormal to Barry Gorge; this was Frank.

Blunt was Barry's sibling.

Their eyes met – Frank more youthful, somewhat taller, and significantly slimmer than Barry was wearing some brilliant, splendid, outside looking garments. Despite the fact that he could never let it out, he was an attractive man and stood certainly before his senior sibling.

Barry and Frank were't the best of siblings; they had battled for their entire lives, everyone accepting that they were superior to the next.

They had similar interests, played similar games yet never conceded to anything.

Straight to the point had left the town when he was mature enough to go all alone.

Straight to the point like Barry was additionally a gourmet specialist and had gone through the most recent 5 years venturing to the far corners of the planet, gathering flavors and flavors from each nation he visited, putting away them in cowhide pockets swinging from his thick calfskin belt.

Barry couldn't tune in to anymore, he didn't need his sibling prodding him about his soup. Forthright proceeded to state how his heart jumped when he saw the princess, how delightful Mariam was, and how enamored he had fallen, however, Barry had vanished upstairs before he could get done with talking.

Straight to the point went through the late evening utilizing the kitchen and extra nourishment to make his perfect work of art – he needed more than anything to intrigue Princess Mariam, he removed his belt and utilized the flavors in enormous amounts to giving the soup an uncommon punch!

Sadly, he was not an incredible gourmet specialist, truth be told, he was very horrendous, yet accepting adoration will discover a way he walked up to the Palace entryways and thumped immovably on the Palace entryway.

As it was so early, just the princess was conscious and meandering the castle.

When Mariam opened the entryway, she right away went gaga for Frank; she had never felt the equivalent about anything (aside from soup obviously).

She welcomed him in and called to her dad without removing her eyes from Frank.

Presently the King was uncertain of Frank; he could see that her little girl was intrigued by this man however manages were rules.

If he was unable to make the best soup on the planet, he would not be permitted to wed Mariam.

As the table was readied and the soup presented, he kept a close eye on Mariam – if this was anything but a phenomenal soup, he would tell.

The soup was warmed and brought to Mariam.

The princess grinned at Frank, and Frank grinned back, passing the bowl to her.

She took out her spoon and dunked it in the soup. She trusted more than whatever it would be the best soup.

At that point, similarly, as she carried the spoon to her mouth… ..the Palace entryway flung open.

"WAIT!!!"

It was Barry… he had been tuning in to Frank the prior night. He had utilized a pinch of Franks flavors to his own formula, and once tried, he had hurried to the royal residence without a moment to spare.

"Honest," he said, "You have an inappropriate soup… this is yours."

Mariam took a gander at the two siblings, and abruptly the two of them looked very familiar..these were the two young men that bailed her out of the solidified lake each one of those years prior.

Candid was confounded. However, his sibling was so tenacious the soup swap was made the King, Mariam, and the entirety of the workers trusted him, and the trade was made.

Barry winked at Frank as he set his soup on the table.

The Princess took the bowl and attempted the soup. Her eyes opened wide, and she channeled as she said, "That is it!!! … The universes best soup".

The King looked carefully and could come clean with his little girl was telling – he could barely handle it.

"Congrats, my Son," he said and put his arm around Frank.

Forthright took Mariam in his arms and requested that she wed him. It didn't take long for an answer…

"Goodness, Yes !!!" and before the month was out, they were hitched.

Straight to the point never comprehended why Barry had acted the hero, maybe he needed to see his sibling glad, maybe he needed to demonstrate that he could make the best soup on the planet… with the correct fixings!

Whatever the explanation, one thing is, without a doubt, they all lived (as regularly they do in these accounts) cheerfully ever after.

CPSIA information can be obtained
at www.ICGtesting.com
Printed in the USA
BVHW061416130421
604817BV00014B/1393